ers
19

"I'm just a human being gifted with the ability to play baseball. I'm nothing special. I'm just another person."

—Robin Yount

Brewers
19
STUBBS
10
Brewers

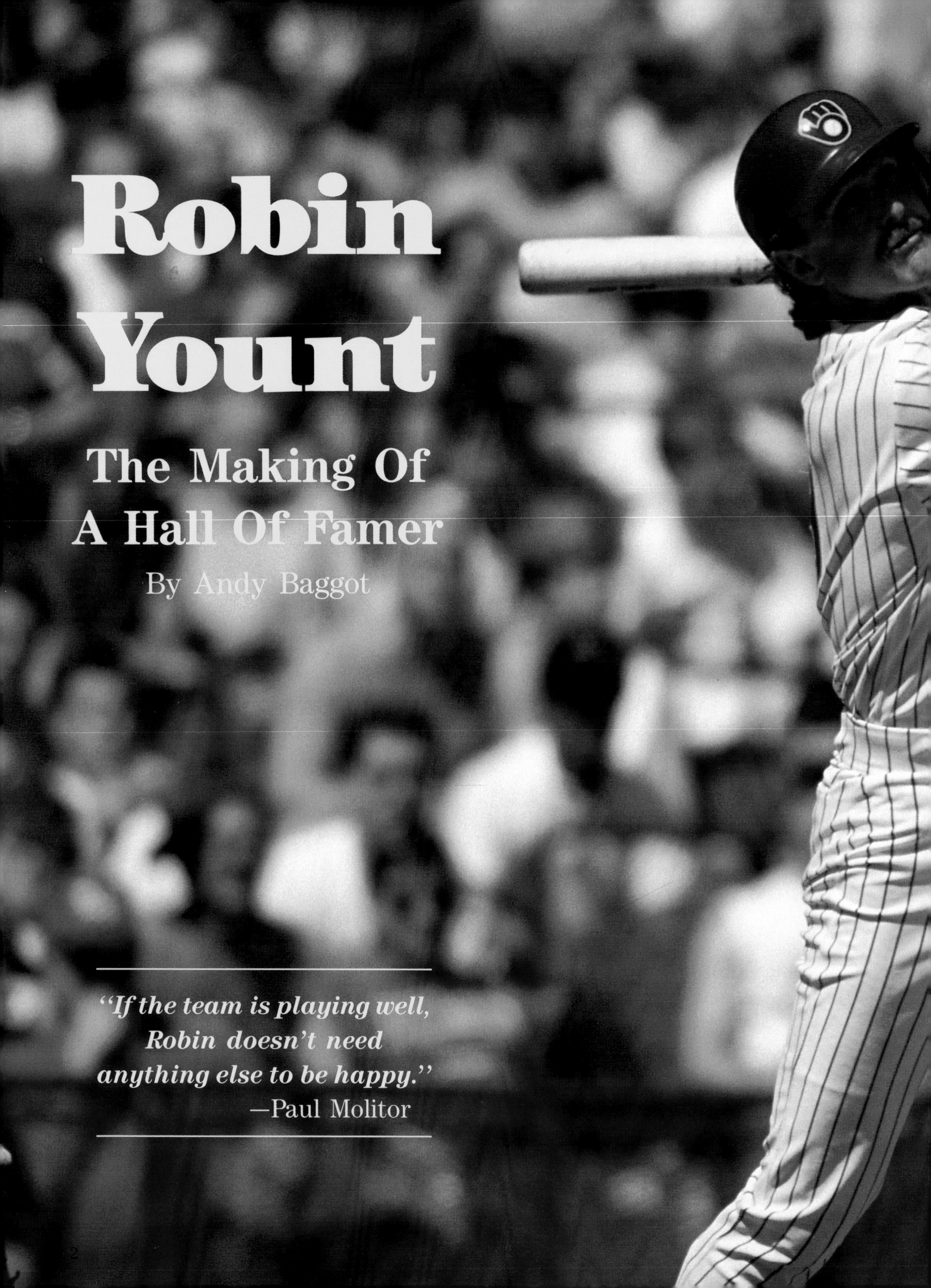

Robin Yount

The Making Of A Hall Of Famer

By Andy Baggot

"If the team is playing well, Robin doesn't need anything else to be happy."
—Paul Molitor

3000

Yount Becomes The 3rd Youngest In Baseball History To Reach Milestone

To find the scenic bluff from where Robin Yount views all the fuss being made over his 3,000th hit, follow this road and make a hard right at unassuming.

"If you play long enough, you're going to get there. It's as simple as that."

Hang a left at humble.

"To me it doesn't mean you're that great a player. It means you've lasted a while. I've played a long time. I don't know that that's a sign of being a great player. Obviously, I've been good enough to stay in the lineup, but that doesn't mean I'm anything great."

Then another right at modest.

"If you go out there enough times, you're going to get 3,000 hits. You don't have to be great to get 3,000 hits. You gotta be good enough to stay in the lineup. You definitely don't have to be great."

Stop the car and get out when you get to unpretentious.

"I'm still here and the numbers are going to add up after a while."

Yount makes it sound so darn simple. As though you could randomly yank a guy off the County Stadium grounds crew, dress him in double knits, put a bat and glove in his hands for 19 major-league seasons, and, eventually, he would reach a milestone reserved almost exclusively for Hall of Famers.

Yount makes it sound so ordinary. As though the one-season efforts of Dick Adkins (one hit for Philadelphia in 1942) and Ken Poulsen (one hit for Boston in 1967) were no more noteworthy and no less honorable.

Yount makes it sound so trivial. As though 3,000 hits is equal in stature to the contributions made by Eddie Gaedel, the midget made famous by the late Bill Veeck.

Of course, it is more than all that. Yount, the Milwaukee Brewers center fielder, resident icon and public treasure since 1974, has earned the right to take his place among legends. Consider:

- Coming into the season, 13,682 men had played in the majors since 1871, but only 16 have preceded Yount to the 3,000-hit plateau. The last was Rod Carew in 1985. Of that group, 15 have been enshrined in the Baseball Hall of Fame in Cooperstown, N.Y.
- Until now, only one other player in history - Willie Mays - has recorded at least 3,000 hits, 200 home runs, 200 stolen bases and 100 triples in his career.
- Only Hall of Famers Ty Cobb, who was 34 years, eight months and one day old, and Henry Aaron, who was 36 years, three months and 12 days old, were younger than Yount when they recorded their 3,000th hit.
- Hall of Famer Stan Musial is the only other member of the 3,000-hit club who has been named his league's most valuable player while playing two different positions.

But while associates assure us that Yount will take pride in his latest accomplishment, he is not being phony when he so cavalierly downplays its significance. He is being himself. Given a hypothetical choice of getting his 3,000th hit or indulging in another passion by driving in the Indianapolis 500, Yount answered quickly. "That would be easy," he said with a laugh. "I'd go drive in the Indy 500. That's just another hit."

"He makes light of this magic number," said longtime friend and Brewers radio announcer Bob Uecker. "But I know when he gets it and when it's over, he'll be a lot happier."

Yount, 36, has never been about records (he holds virtually every club career standard for offensive production), awards (in addition to being voted American League most valuable player in 1982 and '89, he received the team honor in 1982, '87, '88 and '89) and recognition (he has been chosen to play in the All-Star Game three times).

Attempts to weave them into the conversation, postgame or otherwise, are met with a roll of the eyes, a weary sigh and a polite, but speedy dismissal. His lifestyle and actions reflect that attitude.

Rob Deer, a close friend and former teammate, recalled his first visit to the Yount home in Paradise Valley, Arizona, in 1986. Deer was sure he would see trophies, plaques and memorabilia incorporated lavishly in the decor.

"He had a room that had a lot of different trophies, but it was like a big closet in the basement and all this stuff in boxes," said Deer, now with the Detroit Tigers. "I looked at his Gold Glove (which Yount received for being the best fielding shortstop in the American League in 1982) and said, 'Wow, this is the greatest.' He said, 'You want to see something even greater, check this out.' And he showed me this big, huge picture of a race car."

There was the time a plaque of some sort was delivered to Yount in care of the Brewers clubhouse. After looking it over briefly, he unceremoniously handed it to Tony Migliaccio, the clubhouse manager and a good friend, and told him it was his to keep.

When it became apparent after the 1982 World Series season that Yount had an excellent chance to be voted the AL's most valuable player, Brewers Media Relations Director Tom Skibosh told him it might be a good idea to stay near the telephone the day the award was announced. Skibosh said a representative of the Baseball Writers Association of America-whose members' votes determine the winner-needed Yount's home phone number to call and congratulate him.

"Don't give him my number," Yount said.

When it was revealed that Yount was the near-unanimous winner, the representative had to call Skibosh, who in turn called Yount at the previously prescribed time. There was no answer. When he finally answered later in the day, Yount explained he was out grocery shopping with the family.

"People talk about him not really caring about his accomplishments, and that's the honest-to-God truth," Deer said. "He doesn't care about that stuff. The only thing that means anything to him in this game is winning."

Another former teammate, the loquacious Dave Parker, once took inventory of Yount's long, curly, blondish hair and mustache and began calling him "General Custer." Given his preference for the understated, Yount no doubt has felt like the ill-fated cavalry leader during his Summer of '92 pursuit, surrounded by interviewers waiting for a moment of his time and being bombarded by scoreboard updates on his statistical advancements.

While he is not one to decline interviews, Yount did take exception to the practice earlier this season of having almost every statistical step he took blasted over the public address system. One such announcement came just after he had taken his stance in the batter's box. Things were toned down after a meeting with Owner Bud Selig.

Yount said he doesn't pay any attention to the updates that do show up on the scoreboard, but that is not to say he is left completely unaware. First Base Coach Tim Foli made it a point of clipping a section from daily media notes entitled "Yount Count" and putting it under his hat. If and when Yount reaches first, Foli hauls out the sheet and begins to recite for Yount the names of players he has passed, their numbers and their positions on the all-time list.

"I usually have to tell him to shut up," Yount said, a hint of irritation in his voice.

After 19 seasons, the man all his teammates refer to as "Kid" has only one regret.

In 1982, he helped lead the Brewers to the AL East Division title, the league crown and a berth in the World Series, where they lost in seven games to St. Louis.

The singular reason Yount continues to play is so that he might have a chance to get back to the World Series and win.

"That's the only thing I feel like hasn't been accomplished," he said.

It is a goal that shaped his childhood. He grew up in Woodland Hills, California, after Phil Yount moved his wife Marion and sons Larry, Jim and Robin from Danville, Illinois. Robin recalls playing game after game of stick ball with Andy Fransica, a boyhood friend from across the street.

"He and I would play a little baseball game against each other," Yount said. "We were always playing World Series games."

His favorite team was the San Francisco Giants, but Yount doesn't recall emulating a single player. "That's because we went through the lineup," he said. "We were the whole team. We were every guy on that team.

"I've dreamed of being in a World Series ever since I picked up a bat and ball."

But baseball was not the only hobby of his youth. "I love anything with an engine in it," he said.

Yount became hooked on motor sports at an early age and has since raced cars and motorcycles competitively. He has attended professional driving schools in both disciplines and openly admires those who drive fast for a living. Who can forget the civic celebration following the '82 World Series when Yount roared into County Stadium on an off-road motorcycle?

ROBIN YOUNT
HIT PARADE - CAREER MILESTONES

HIT	DATE	OPPONENT	PITCHER	SCORE	HIT/INNING
1	April 12, 1974	Baltimore	Dave McNally	5-3 L	Single/4th
500	July 10, 1977	Boston	Luis Tiant	8-5 L	Single/6th
1000	August 16, 1980	at Cleveland	Sandy Wihtol	10-5 W	Double/4th
1500	August 25, 1983	California	Tommy John	7-0 W	Double/5th
2000	September 6, 1986	Cleveland	Don Schulze	17-9 L	Single/7th
2500	July 2, 1989	at New York	Jimmy Jones	10-2 W	Single/5th
3000	September 9, 1992	Cleveland	Jose Mesa	5-4 L	Single/7th

EASTON

"As far back as I can remember, I picture my dad listening to the Indy 500 on the radio," Yount said. "Some seed was planted that motor sports was pretty neat stuff."

The affair officially began with motorcylces when Yount was 13 or 14. "A friend of my brother's was interested in it and he had some friends, high school age guys, that were doing that," he recalled. "I got to tag along one time to some motocross races. I went one time and I was pretty convinced that's what I wanted to do."

There is a story behind the acquisition of his first bike. After returning from his first season as a pitcher in the Houston Astros farm system, Larry purchased a small conservative motorcycle to get around town on.

"When he went away the next summer to play pro ball, he left it in the garage and I just sort of tore all the street stuff off it and made it into a racing bike," Robin said.

"I kind of inherited that one. When he got back, it was in no condition for him to ride on the street anymore, so I guess in that respect, he bought me one.

"He wasn't crazy about it, but there wasn't much he could do. It was shot for what he wanted to do."

Accompanied by his father, Yount soon began entering motorcycle races around Southern California. The attraction was strong enough that, for a time, baseball was not a priority.

"Baseball was not a goal during high school," Yount said. "I was having a heck of a lot of fun racing."

That would soon change, though.

How would life be different for Yount had things turned out the way he anticipated in 1973?

A 17-year-old shortstop from Taft High School, Yount was drafted by the Brewers third overall that year behind pitcher David Clyde (Texas) and catcher John Stearns (Philadelphia).

Judging from the way scouts were talking, Yount believed he would go to the club that picked fourth.

The San Diego Padres wound up taking Dave Winfield instead.

Clyde, a teenage sensation, was rushed to the major leagues by Rangers Owner Bob Short against the advice of his scouts. A left-hander, Clyde soon developed arm problems, played five seasons and never compiled a winning record.

Stearns, a standout college football player at Colorado, lasted 11 major-league seasons, 10 with the New York Mets. He finished 2,304 hits shy of 3,000.

Yount, meanwhile, reportedly received a $75,000 signing bonus to join the Brewers. After spending one season in the minors - he hit .285 in 64 rookie league games at Newark of the New York-Pennsylvania League - Manager Del Crandall had Yount in the opening day lineup April 5, 1974 against Boston. At the time, he was the youngest everyday player in the major leagues.

Some perspective: Yount said his first major-league salary was $15,500. The daily per diem for road trips was less than $15. He signed his first baseball card "Rob Yount." He lived downtown at the Astor Hotel on Juneau Avenue.

Yount hit .250 that first year. He also committed 44 errors, a club record that still stands.

In retrospect, Yount said the circumstances in Milwaukee were perfect for his development. "I was brought into a situation where there was really no pressure to perform at anything more than a learning-situation level," he said.

"For the mere fact of surroundings and everything, no matter how many years you play in the minor leagues, you still need a couple of years' learning experience from the point when you finally get to the major leagues. Here I was, getting all that at an early age. I mean, here I was just thrown out there to play shortstop, and that's what I did. I wasn't concerned with going up or down or whatever."

In terms of developing confidence and poise, it helped, too, that Yount had been exposed to the ebb and flow of professional baseball while still in high school. On two occasions, Robin recalls visiting his brother Larry and working out with him during homestands while Larry was at Class AAA Oklahoma City.

"It definitely gave me an advantage of knowing what it was like before I ever did it," Yount said.

It was in the spring of 1978 and a combination of factors had come together to make Yount seriously consider quitting baseball.

One, he had injured an ankle in a motorcycle mishap about a month before the start of spring training.

Two, he came to camp in Sun City, Arizona, still feeling the effects of the injury and was unable to compete at full-tilt.

Three, and this was the most telling circumstance, is that Yount was disillusioned. During his first four seasons in the majors, the Brewers had compiled a cumulative record of 277-370, finished a combined 108 games out of first place and never placed higher than fifth under managers Crandall and Alex Grammas.

"The combination made me wonder if this is really what I wanted to do," Yount said.

Rumors began circulating that he was on the verge of retiring and was contemplating a career in professional golf.

"It was just a matter of, 'If this is all there is to this game, maybe there's other things I can do,' " Yount said of the golf talk. "It just wasn't that exciting finishing fifth and sixth every year. That didn't do a whole lot for me."

His attitude would change. Between 1978 and '82, Milwaukee finished no lower than third, averaged 21 games over .500, and won divisional crowns in '81 and '82. That, Yount said, rekindled his spirit.

In essence, this scenario best describes the way Yount lives his competitive life. His ultimate motivation is not fame or money. It is the promise that if you put forth your best effort, hold

Your Local Coca-Cola Bottler
Congratulates Robin Yount
on his 3000th hit.
Enjoy Coca-Cola Trademarks ® CLASSIC
Can't Beat
The Real Thing.
Enjoy Coca-Cola CLASSIC
WISCONSIN PROUD
SPOKEN HERE
© 1992 The Coca-Cola Company. "Coca-Cola" and the Dynamic Ribbon device are registered trademarks of The Coca-Cola Company.

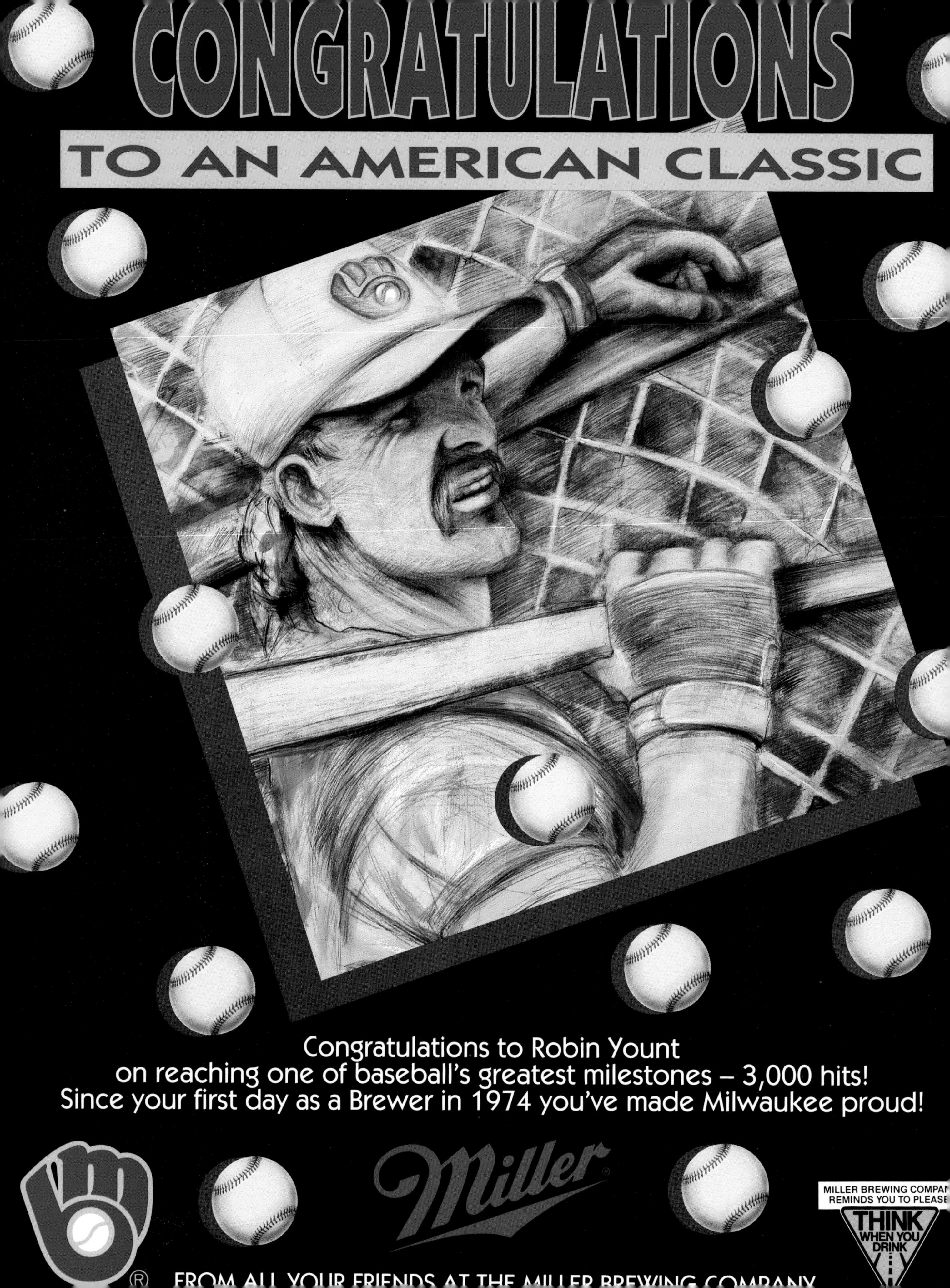

CONGRATULATIONS
TO AN AMERICAN CLASSIC
Congratulations to Robin Yount
on reaching one of baseball's greatest milestones – 3,000 hits!
Since your first day as a Brewer in 1974 you've made Milwaukee proud!
Miller
MILLER BREWING COMPAN
REMINDS YOU TO PLEASE
THINK
WHEN YOU
DRINK
FROM ALL YOUR FRIENDS AT THE MILLER BREWING COMPANY

absolutely nothing back, you can find fulfillment. In turn, if 25 men can come together with a similiar mindset, you have the makings of a great, championship-calibre team.

"Everyone talks about putting the team first," said infielder/designated hitter Paul Molitor, whose arrival in 1978 coincided with the franchise's resurgence. "It's easy to say, but Robin is one ballplayer who can say it with absolute honesty. His goals have nothing to do with hitting .300, or getting 100 RBI. If the team is playing well, Robin doesn't need anything else to be happy."

Yount has endured operations on his right shoulder in 1984 and '85 which prompted his move from shortstop to center field. He has played games despite a cracked bone in his finger and a bruised knee so bloated with fluid former manager Tom Trebelhorn said, "it looked like someone stuffed a ball in there."

As long as he is able to put on his uniform, swing a bat and throw a baseball, Yount believes he should be in the lineup.

Yount said the biggest change he has noticed among his peers over the years is how they have geared their expectations and performances around their individual statistics.

"That obviously has to do with the money involved," said Yount, who in 1989 signed a three-year, $9.6-million contract.

"You're talking such great sums of money to be made as a player. Basically, that sum is determined by the numbers you're able to put up. In turn, the focus of today's players may be more statistical-minded than it once was."

There was a time, Yount said, when getting to the World Series and winning it provided the greatest monetary reward a player could receive.

"Now, if you don't personally - out of self-pride or team pride - have that will to win, it's not the No. 1 goal anymore necessarily."

Yount admits to being overwhelmed by his salary. "I'm making a ton, there's no doubt about that," he said. "More than I could ever have dreamed of making, it's mind-boggling to me to think of the money we make these days."

Which is why he finds it hard to blame players for their change in attitudes.

"I'm not faulting the player," he said. "When you can make as much money as you can in this game, it's pretty difficult to fault somebody for thinking that way.

"The only problem I have with it, is normally if everyone plays good enough as a team to win, everyone's numbers will be there and the money will come."

Yount has always been intensely private in matters regarding his life and time away from the ballpark. When asked if he would sit down for an hour or so and be interviewed at his hotel on the road, he declined saying he couldn't imagine answering questions for so long.

"That's pretty much the way I've been," said Yount, whose brother Larry handles his contract matters. "As far as the game of baseball goes, that's in the public eye. But I don't think one's personal life has to be. I've never been one to expose it anymore than I have to."

Yount and wife Michele have four children, Melissa, Amy, Jenna and Dustin. They live in Hales Corners during the season.

"A lot of it has to do with my family," said Yount, who refused to have his family pictured in a Sports Illustrated story about him two years ago. "It's tough enough for kids to grow up these days let alone have everybody knowing and seeing and watching what you do and knowing who you are. I basically want them to grow up with as normal a life as possible."

Virtually everything about Yount is understated, from the clothes he wears to the polite, sincere way he deals with the public. His style probably has prevented him from being voted to a few more All-Star teams, but it has not stopped those who compete against him from noticing and professing their admiration.

"I love the way Robin Yount plays the game," Boston Red Sox pitcher Frank Viola said. "You watch teams come and go. Nobody hustles like he does. He goes hard every play, every at-bat. He does everything you could ask of a guy. He's a film on how you should play the game."

Perhaps Detroit Sparky Anderson said it best, though. "He's going to be a Hall of Famer, no question about that. He'll reach 3,000 hits, no question about that. But to be able to do all this without making any noise to me is the proudest thing he will have when he retires."

3,000 HITS
MAJOR LEAGUE HISTORY
AGE CHART

As of September 9, 1992

PLAYER	DATE	AGE	CAREER/HITS
Ty Cobb	August 19, 1921	34 Years, 8 Months, 01 Days	24 Yrs/4,191
Henry Aaron	May 17, 1970	36 Years, 3 Months, 12 Days	23 Yrs/3,771
ROBIN YOUNT	**September 9, 1992**	**36 Years, 11 Months, 24 Days**	**19 Yrs/3,000**
Pete Rose	May 5, 1978	37 Years, 0 Months, 21 Days	24 Yrs/4,256
Tris Speaker	May 17, 1925	37 Years, 1 Months, 13 Days	22 Yrs/3,515
Stan Musial	May 13, 1958	37 Years, 5 Months, 22 Days	22 Yrs/3,630
Eddie Collins	June 6, 1925	38 Years, 1 Months, 01 Days	25 Yrs/3,311
Roberto Clemente	September 30, 1972	38 Years, 1 Months, 12 Days	18 Yrs/3,000
Paul Waner	June 19, 1942	39 Years, 2 Months, 03 Days	20 Yrs/3,152
Willie Mays	July 18, 1970	39 Years, 2 Months, 12 Days	22 Yrs/3,283
Al Kaline	September 24, 1974	39 Years, 9 Months, 05 Days	22 Yrs/3,007
Rod Carew	August 4, 1985	39 Years, 10 Months, 03 Days	19 Yrs/3,053
Carl Yastrzemski	September 12, 1979	40 Years, 0 Months, 21 Days	23 Yrs/3,419
Nap Lajoie	September 27, 1914	40 Years, 0 Months, 22 Days	21 Yrs/3,251
Lou Brock	August 13, 1979	40 Years, 1 Months, 25 Days	19 Yrs/3,023
Honus Wagner	June 9, 1914	40 Years, 3 Months, 13 Days	21 Yrs./3,430
Cap Anson	July 18, 1897	46 Years, 2 Months, 07 Days	22 Yrs/3,041

The 3000
Baseball's All-Time

CAP ANSON

Cap Anson

Born: April 17, 1852 — Marshalltown, Iowa
Died: April 14, 1922 — Chicago, Illinois

Elected to Hall of Fame in 1939

Playing Career: Rockford Forest Citys (NA*) 1871
Philadelphia Athletics (NA*) 1872-75
Chicago Cubs (NL) 1876-97 **National Association*

Manager: Chicago Cubs (NL) 1879-97
New York Giants (NL) 1898

Known as ''Pop'' . . . First player to collect 3,000 hits . . . He also was the oldest (46 years, 2 months, 7 days) to attain it . . . Accomplished the feat on July 18, 1897 . . . It was a fourth inning single . . . The feat never made the Chicago newspapers . . . Anson was the foremost on-field baseball figure of the 19th century . . . Led the National League in hitting three times (1879, 1881 & 1888) . . . Was the first to hit .400 twice (.407 in 1879 and .421 in 1887) . . . Was the first to hit three successive home runs in a game (1884) and four doubles in a game (1883) . . . As a manager, led Chicago to 15 first-division finishes, including pennants in 1880, '81, '82, '85 and '86.

Playing Career	AVG.	G	AB	R	H	2B	3B	HR	RBI	BB	SO	SB
22 Years	.334	2276	9108	1719	3041	532	124	96	1715	952	294	247

HONUS WAGNER

Honus Wagner

Born: February 24, 1874 — Carnegie, Pennsylvania
Died: December 6, 1955 — Carnegie, Pennsylvania

Elected to Hall of Fame in 1936

Playing Career: Louisville (NL) 1897-99
Pittsburgh Pirates (NL) 1900-17

Manager: Pittsburgh Pirates (NL) 1917

Known as the ''Flying Dutchman'' . . . Considered the greatest all-around player . . . Played at every position except catcher . . . Broke into the major leagues with a .344 batting average in 1897 and produced 17 straight .330-plus seasons, including eight National League batting titles . . . Was the first player to have his signature on a Louisville Slugger (1905) baseball bat . . . His 1909 baseball card is worth over $100,000 . . . A flawless fielder, he was a brilliant base-runner, amassing 722 stolen bases, topping the league in thefts six times . . . Collected his 3,000th hit, a double, on June 9, 1914 . . . Managed for only five games . . . Returning in 1933, was a Pirates coach until 1951, tutoring such future Hall of Famers as Pie Traynor, Kiki Cuyler, Arky Vaughn, Ralph Kiner and the Waner brothers, Paul and Lloyd . . . Was one of the original five players (Ty Cobb, Babe Ruth, Christy Mathewson and Walter Johnson) elected to the Hall of Fame.

Playing Career	AVG.	G	AB	R	H	2B	3B	HR	RBI	BB	SO	SB
21 Years	.329	2786	10427	1740	3430	651	252	101	1732	963	327	722

Hit Club

Leading Hitters

NAP LAJOIE

Nap Lajoie

Born: September 5, 1874 – Woonsocket, Rhode Island
Died: February 7, 1959 – Daytona Beach, Florida

Elected to Hall of Fame in 1937

Playing Career: Philadelphia Phillies (NL) 1896-1901
Philadelphia Athletics (AL) 1901-02; 1915-16
Cleveland Indians (AL) 1902-14

Manager: Cleveland Indians (AL) 1905-09

Considered the greatest second baseman to ever play the game . . . Topped the .300 mark 16 times, including 10 times over .350 . . . Won three batting crowns during his day, including .422 in his first American League campaign . . . During the dead-ball era, was known as a powerful pull-hitter, collecting 893 extra base hits . . . On September 15, 1914, became the first American League player to reach the 3,000 hit plateau . . . A fan favorite, he was a player-manager for five seasons and the club was called the "Naps" in his honor . . . Was the sixth player elected to the Hall of Fame.

Playing Career	AVG.	G	AB	R	H	2B	3B	HR	RBI	BB	SO	SB
21 Years	.339	2475	9589	1504	3251	648	163	82	1599	516	85	395

TY COBB

Ty Cobb

Born: December 18, 1886 – Narrows, Georgia
Died: July 17, 1961 – Atlanta, Georgia

Elected to Hall of Fame in 1936

Playing Career: Detroit Tigers (AL) 1905-26
Philadelphia Athletics (AL) 1927-28

Manager: Detroit Tigers (AL) 1921-26

Known as the "Georgia Peach" . . . Arguably, the greatest player to play the game . . . Was considered one of the game's fiercest competitors . . . Won the first of a record 12 batting championships at age 20 . . . Batted .400 or better three times . . . In 1909, he was the first player to win the Triple Crown . . . In 1911, set the American League record when he hit safely in 41 consecutive games, now the 4th longest batting streak in modern day history . . . Also was named the Most Valuable Player in 1911 . . . Is the youngest player (34 years, 8 months, 1 day) to reach the 3,000 hit level, accomplishing the feat on August 19, 1921 . . . When he retired, after 24 years, he held more than 90 major league records . . . His lifetime .367 batting average is a major league record . . . Holds the record with 50 career steals of home plate . . . Three other significant records—his 4,191 hits, 96 steals in 1915 and 892 career stolen bases—withstood the test of time for more than 50 years . . . As one of the original five players inducted to Baseball's Hall of Fame, he was the top-vote getter, receiving 222 of a possible 226 ballots, seven more than Babe Ruth and Honus Wagner.

Playing Career	AVG.	G	AB	R	H	2B	3B	HR	RBI	BB	SO	SB
24 Years	.367	3034	11429	2245	4191	724	297	118	1961	1249	357	892

MILWAUKEE'S HOMETOWN AIRLINE SALUTES A HOMETOWN HERO.

TRIS SPEAKER

Tris Speaker

Born: April 4, 1888 — Hubbard, Texas
Died: December 8, 1958 — Lake Whitney, Texas

Elected to Hall of Fame in 1937

Playing Career: Boston Red Sox (AL) 1907-15
Cleveland Indians (AL) 1916-26
Washington Senators (AL) 1927
Philadelphia Athletics (AL) 1928

Manager: Cleveland Indians (AL) 1919-26

Known as the "Gray Eagle" . . . Revolutionized outfield play by positioning himself in shallow centerfield . . . As a rookie, Cy Young would hit him fly balls to sharpen his ability . . . Holds the major league record with 449 assists from the outfield . . . On his Hall of Fame plaque there is an inscription that reads "greatest centerfielder of his day" . . . Incredibly won only one batting title during his career, despite a .344 lifetime average . . . He is the all-time leader with 793 career doubles, leading the American League eight times in that category . . . In 1912, he won the A.L. home run title and was named the league's Most Valuable Player . . . He also ranks fifth in hits, seventh in triples and eighth in runs scored . . . Collected his 3,000th career hit on May 17, 1925 . . . As the player-manager, he led the Cleveland Indians to their first World Series title in 1920 . . . The seventh player elected to the Hall of Fame.

Playing Career	AVG.	G	AB	R	H	2B	3B	HR	RBI	BB	SO	SB
22 Years	.344	2789	10208	1881	3515	793	223	117	1559	1381	220	433

EDDIE COLLINS

Eddie Collins

Born: May 2, 1887 — Millerton, New York
Died: March 25, 1951 — Boston, Massachusetts

Elected to Hall of Fame in 1939

Playing Career: Philadelphia Athletics (AL) 1906-14
Chicago White Sox (AL) 1915-26
Philadelphia Athletics (AL) 1927-30

Manager: Chicago White Sox (AL) 1925-26

Known as "Cocky" . . . An aggressive and confident second baseman, he was known for his outstanding ability to steal bases . . . Holds the American League record with 25 years of service . . . Although he never won a batting title, he batted better than .340 on 10 occasions . . . He was one of the first players to use a choke grip batting style . . . Topped the American League four times in stolen bases and nine times led all second basemen in fielding . . . Played on six World Series teams, including the infamous 1919 Chicago "Black Sox" . . . Not involved in the scandal, he was unforgiving of his teammates who were guilty of "fixing" the series against the Cincinnati Reds . . . On June 6, 1925, he doubled off Detroit's Walter Johnson for his 3,000th career hit . . . After retiring, he joined high school friend Tom Yawkey as a part-time General Manager . . . Was credited for scouting prospects Bobby Doerr and Ted Williams.

Playing Career	AVG.	G	AB	R	H	2B	3B	HR	RBI	BB	SO	SB
25 Years	.333	2826	9949	1818	3311	437	187	47	1299	1503	286	743

We Give You Tomorrow's Hall of Famers

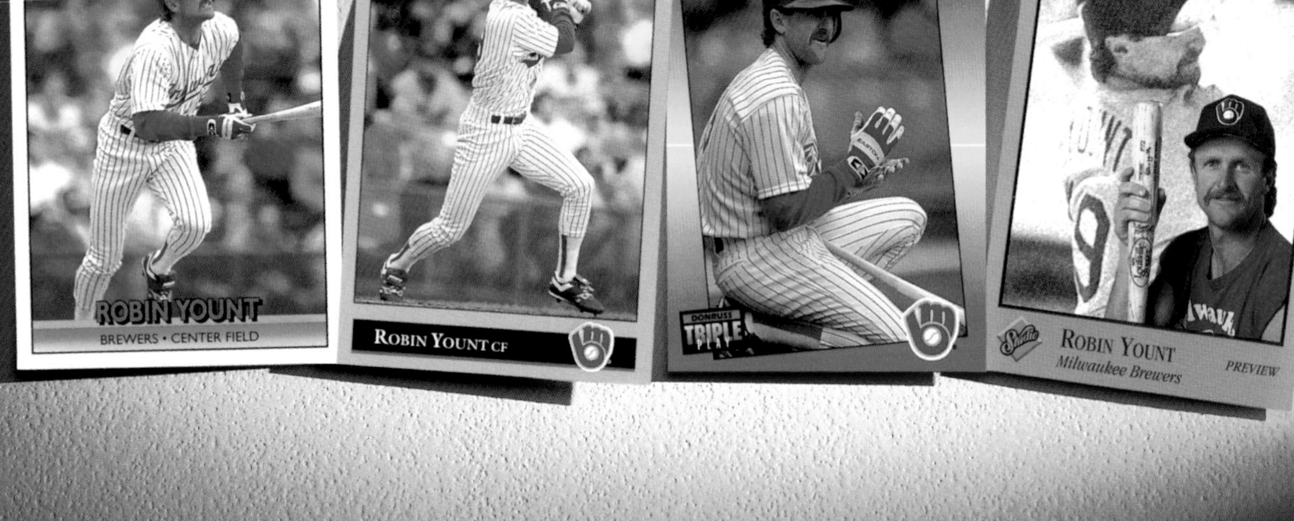
DONRUSS 1992
ROBIN YOUNT
BREWERS • CENTER FIELD
Leaf
ROBIN YOUNT CF
ROBIN YOUNT
CF
DONRUSS
TRIPLE PLAY
Studio
ROBIN YOUNT
Milwaukee Brewers
PREVIEW

MAJOR LEAGUE
BASEBALL
LEAF SET
BASEBALL
15 CARDS
1992
EDITION

Today.

1992 PREMIER EDITION
DONRUSS
TRIPLE
PLAY
15 BASEBALL CARDS
AND A TRIPLE PLAY GAME CARD
Studio
PREMIUM QUALITY
BASEBALL CARDS

©MLBPA,1992

Congratulations, Robin, on your 3,000th career hit.

PAUL WANER

Paul Waner

Born: April 16, 1903 — Harrah, Oklahoma
Died: August 29, 1965 — Sarasota, Florida

Elected to Hall of Fame in 1952

Playing Career: Pittsburgh Pirates (NL) 1926-40
Brooklyn Dodgers (NL) 1941; 1943-44
Boston Braves (NL) 1941-42
New York Yankees (AL) 1944-45

Known as ''Big Poison'' . . . Older brother of Lloyd ''Little Poison'', who was elected to the Hall of Fame in 1967 . . . Paul was a speedy outfielder with a rifle throwing arm, perhaps possessing the strongest throwing arm seen in Pittsburgh until Roberto Clemente . . . A line drive hitter who won three National League batting titles while topping the .300 plateau 14 times during his career . . . In 1927, he led the Pirates to the N.L. pennant by batting .380 with 237 hits, 17 triples and 131 RBI, earning his only league Most Valuable Player award . . . A 3-time All-Star . . . While in the twilight of his career with the Boston Braves, he became the sixth player to compile 3,000 career hits, accomplishing the feat on June 19, 1942.

Playing Career	AVG.	G	AB	R	H	2B	3B	HR	RBI	BB	SO	SB
20 Years	.333	2549	9459	1626	3152	603	190	112	1309	1091	376	104

STAN MUSIAL

Stan Musial

Born: November 21, 1920 — Donora, Pennsylvania

Elected to Hall of Fame in 1969

Playing Career: St. Louis Cardinals (NL) 1941-63

Known as ''Stan the Man'' . . . The first genuine power-hitter to surpass the 3,000 hit level . . . He accomplished the feat on May 13, 1958 . . . Noted for his compressed, closed stance . . . One of the more consistent hitters to play the game, he had 1,815 hits at home and 1,815 hits on the road . . . He scored 1,949 runs and drove in another 1,951 runs . . . he amassed 1377 extra base hits, ranking among the majors all-time leaders in doubles, triples and home runs . . . A 3-time National League Most Valuable Player, he is one of only 3 players (Detroit's Hank Greenberg and Milwaukee Brewers' Robin Yount) to ever earn the distinction at two different positions . . . Batted better than .300 18 times during his career, leading the N.L. in batting seven times, including in three consecutive seasons . . . Topped the league in doubles eight times, in hits six times, in triples and runs scored five times . . . A member of 24 N.L. All-Star teams, he is most remembered for hitting a 12th inning homer to win the 1955 mid-summer classic at County Stadium . . . In 1956, *The Sporting News* named him the first ''Player of the Decade'' . . . When he retired, he owned or shared 29 N.L. records, 17 major league marks and six All-Star Game records.

Playing Career	AVG.	G	AB	R	H	2B	3B	HR	RBI	BB	SO	SB
22 Years	.331	3026	10972	1949	3630	725	177	475	1951	1599	696	78

PABST BREWING CO.
SINCE 1844
Highest Quality
Established in Milwaukee 1844
Pabst
Blue Ribbon
BEER
12 FL. OZ. (354 ml)

There's only one way to salute a star.

PBR me ASAP

Congratulations Robin!

Pabst Brewing Company, Milwaukee, WI.

HENRY AARON

Hank Aaron

Born: February 5, 1934 — Mobile, Alabama

Elected to Hall of Fame in 1982

Playing Career: Milwaukee Braves (NL) 1954-65
Atlanta Braves (NL) 1966-74
Milwaukee Brewers (AL) 1975-76

Known as ''Hammerin' Hank'' . . . The all-time home run king with 755 homers . . . On April 8, 1974, he entered the record book with his 715th home run, surpassing Babe Ruth . . . He accomplished the feat off Los Angeles' Al Downing in Atlanta . . . Aaron also set all-time records in total bases, extra base hits and runs batted in; second in at bats and runs scored and third in games played . . . Hit 40 or more home runs on eight occasions while driving in 100 or more runs a dozen times in a season . . . Is the second youngest player (36 years, 4 months, 12 days) to collect his 3,000th career hit, that coming on May 17, 1970 . . . By doing so, he was the first to reach that plateau in 12 years . . . He led the National League in batting twice, home runs and RBI four times . . . Was named *The Sporting News* ''Player of the Year'' in 1956 and 1963 . . . 3-time Gold Glove outfielder . . . In 1957, he led the Milwaukee Braves to their only World Championship, earning the N.L.'s Most Valuable Player award . . . Played in 24 All-Star Games . . . Spent all but two seasons with the Braves, first in Milwaukee and later in Atlanta . . . Closed out his career with the Milwaukee Brewers, hitting his final 22 homers in the American League . . . His final home run came on July 20, 1976 off California's Dick Drago at County Stadium . . . He became the Brewers' first player inducted to the Hall of Fame . . . The Brewers retired his uniform number 44 following the 1976 season.

Playing Career	AVG.	G	AB	R	H	2B	3B	HR	RBI	BB	SO	SB
23 Years	.305	3298	12364	2174	3771	624	98	755	2297	1402	1383	240

WILLIE MAYS

Willie Mays

Born: May 6, 1931 — Westfield, Alabama

Elected to Hall of Fame in 1979

Playing Career: New York Giants (NL) 1951-57
San Francisco Giants (NL) 1958-72
New York Mets (NL) 1972-73

Known as ''The Say Hey Kid'' . . . Judged as perhaps the greatest player of all-time . . . A paradigm of the complete player; he could hit for power and average, steal bases, play the field and throw the baseball . . . Along with Henry Aaron and Mickey Mantle, Mays was one of the top sluggers in the game during the 1950's and 1960's . . . An electrifying talent, he was named the 1951 National League Rookie of the Year . . . His totals rank on baseball's all-time list, including third in homers, fifth in home runs scored and seventh in RBI . . . A 2-time Most Valuable Player, he led the National League in home runs four times . . . Ironically, he won just one batting title, that coming in 1954, despite hitting over .300 10 times during his career . . . That season, he led the Giants to the World Series, one of four he played in . . . That World Series is remembered for his spectacular over the shoulder catch of Vic Wertz' deep fly ball . . . Mays drove in 100 or more runs 10 times with a career best 141 in 1962 . . . He managed to hit 51 homers in 1955 and 52 homers in 1965, becoming one of only five players (Babe Ruth, Jimmie Foxx, Ralph Kiner and Mickey Mantle) to hit 50 or more homers more that once . . . He collected his 3,000th career hit on July 18, 1970 . . . Mays also won 4 consecutive stolen base crowns, 11 Gold Gloves and appeared in a record tying 24 All-Star Games.

Playing Career	AVG.	G	AB	R	H	2B	3B	HR	RBI	BB	SO	SB
24 Years	.302	2992	10881	2062	3283	523	140	660	1903	1463	1526	338

PETE ROSE

Pete Rose

Born: April 14, 1941 — Cincinnati, Ohio

Playing Career: Cincinnati Reds (NL) 1963-78; 1985-86
Philadelphia Phillies (NL) 1979-83
Montreal Expos (NL) 1984

Manager: Cincinnati Reds (NL) 1984-89

Known as ''Charlie Hustle'' . . . A player's player . . . No one played the game with the same fervor as he . . . Unquestionably, the greatest switch-hitter ever . . . Two of his trademarks were his head-first slides and sprinting to first base when issued a base-on-balls . . . Played in more seasons than any other National League player . . . In his later years, was noted for bouncing the baseball on the artificial turf when recording the final putout of an inning . . . The all-time hit leader, surpassing Ty Cobb's record many felt would never be broken . . . He established the all-time hit record on September 11, 1985 when he singled off San Diego's Eric Show at Riverfront Stadium . . . Also holds the all-time marks in singles, games played and at bats while he is runner-up in doubles and fourth in runs scored . . . He is the only player to collect at least 100 hits in his first 23 seasons while setting the standard with ten 200-hit campaigns . . . While hitting better than .300, 15 times, he captured three National League batting titles . . . Rose is the only player to ever play at least 500 games at five different positions . . . Named the 1963 Rookie of the Year . . . Ten years later, he earned the N.L. Most Valuable Player award after winning his final batting title and collecting a career best 230 hits . . . One of the youngest players (37 years, 0 months, 21 days) to reach the 3,000 hit class . . . He accomplished that feat on May 5, 1978 . . . That same season, he set the National League modern day record with a 44-game hitting streak, second in baseball history to Joe DiMaggio's legendary 56-game streak set in 1941 . . . Named *The Sporting News* ''Player of the Decade'' for the 1970's . . . Won a pair of Gold Gloves . . . Played in 22 All-Star Games, but will be best remembered for the 1970 Classic when he scored the winning run for the Nationals by crashing into A.L. catcher Ray Fosse in the 12th inning . . . Rose sparked the Cincinnati Reds' ''Big Red Machine'' to four pennants and back-to-back World Championships in 1975 and 1976 . . . In 1980, he helped the Philadelphia Phillies capture their first World Championship . . . A throw-back to the early-days of the game, he became a player-manager with the Reds in 1984.

Playing Career	AVG.	G	AB	R	H	2B	3B	HR	RBI	BB	SO	SB
24 Years	.303	3562	14053	2165	4256	746	135	160	1314	1566	1143	198

LOU BROCK

Lou Brock

Born: June 18, 1939 — El Dorado, Arkansas

Elected to Hall of Fame in 1985

Playing Career: Chicago Cubs (NL) 1961-64
St. Louis Cardinals (NL) 1964-79

The greatest base stealer in National League history . . . Holds the N.L. record with 938 career steals and 118 in a season (1974) . . . Rickey Henderson holds the major league marks, surpassing the 1,000 career total this season and establishing the single season standard of 130 in 1982 . . . Although famous for his speed, Brock did have some power, hitting a 500-foot home run at the old Polo Grounds on June 17, 1962 . . . The fleet-footed outfielder was the National League base stealing leader eight times during a nine year period and swiped 50 or more bases in a season 12 consecutive years . . . He also batted better than .300 eight times during his career, just missing by a mere three percentage points or less on three other occasions . . . Four times during his career he amassed 200 hits . . . Twice he led the league in runs scored while also finding himself atop the leader board in doubles and triples . . . A 4-time All-Star, he led the St. Louis Cardinals to three National League pennants and the 1964 and 1967 World Championship . . . Before retiring following the 1979 season, he became the last National League player to attain 3,000 career hits . . . Brock accomplished the feat on August 13, 1979 against the Chicago Cubs, the only other team he ever played for.

Playing Career	AVG.	G	AB	R	H	2B	3B	HR	RBI	BB	SO	SB
19 Years	.293	2616	10332	1610	3023	486	141	149	900	761	1730	938

ROBERTO CLEMENTE

Born: August 18, 1934 — Carolina, Puerto Rico
Died: December 31, 1972 — San Juan, Puerto Rico

Elected to Hall of Fame in 1973

Playing Career: Pittsburgh Pirates (NL) 1955-72

Roberto Clemente

Admired for his intensity for the game . . . Spectacular defensive talent, noted for having a strong throwing arm, exceptional range and an uncanny ability to make leaping and diving catches . . . Won 12 consecutive Gold Gloves as a rightfielder and set a major league record by leading the National League in assists five times . . . Offensively, batted better than .300, 13 times during his career, including eight straight seasons in which he hit over .312 . . . Five times he batted over .340 . . . Won four batting titles, batting .351 in 1961 and a career high .357 in 1967 . . . Was named the National League Most Valuable Player in 1966 . . . He was named to the N.L. All-Star team 14 times during his career . . . Played in a pair of World Series and earned the 1971 World Series MVP honor in perhaps the greatest individual performance ever . . . In that Fall Classic against Baltimore, he played like a man possessed, making sensational throws and catches while batting .414 with a pair of home runs, including a game winner in Game Seven . . . On September 30, 1972, a fourth inning double off the New York Mets Jon Matlack at Three Rivers Stadium marked his 3,000th hit—it also would he his last . . . On New Year's Eve of 1972, Clemente died in a plane crash while flying relief supplies to Nicaraguan earthquake victims . . . The mandatory five-year waiting period for Hall of Fame induction was waived for Clemente, who was elected in 1973.

Playing Career	AVG.	G	AB	R	H	2B	3B	HR	RBI	BB	SO	SB
18 Years	.317	2433	9454	1416	3000	440	166	240	1305	621	1230	83

AL KALINE

Born: December 19, 1934 — Baltimore, Maryland

Elected to Hall of Fame in 1980

Playing Career: Detroit Tigers (AL) 1953-74

Al Kaline

Known as "Mr. Tiger" . . . A model of consistency . . . Ranks among Detroit's all-time leaders in virtually every offensive category, including topping the list in games played and home runs . . . Joined the Tigers at the tender age of 18 . . . Became the second youngest player to ever hit a grand slam home run . . . Batted over .300 nine times in his career . . . Won just one batting title, that coming in 1955 when he hit a career best .340 . . . At age 20, he was the youngest player to ever win a batting crown . . . It also was the only season he collected 200 hits . . . Finished second to Yogi Berra in the American League Most Valuable Player balloting . . . Became a perennial All-Star, playing in 15 mid-summer classics, including 13 straight from 1955-67 . . . Won 10 Gold Gloves . . . Played in just one World Series . . . Led the Tigers to the 1968 World Championship in a classic seven game confrontation with the St. Louis Cardinals . . . Rallied the Tigers from a 3-games-to-1 deficit by batting .379 with a pair of home runs and eight RBI . . . He reached the 3,000 hit plateau on September 24, 1974 . . . After retiring, he moved to the Tigers' broadcast booth.

Playing Career	AVG.	G	AB	R	H	2B	3B	HR	RBI	BB	SO	SB
22 Years	.297	2834	10116	1622	3007	498	75	399	1583	1277	1020	137

CARL YASTRZEMSKI

Born: August 22, 1939 — Southampton, New York

Elected to Hall of Fame in 1989

Playing Career: Boston Red Sox (AL) 1961-83

Carl Yastrzemski

Known as "Yaz" . . . Replaced the legendary Ted Williams in leftfield, then followed him to Cooperstown . . . Boston's all-time leader in games played, at bats, runs, hits, doubles, total bases, runs batted in and extra base hits . . . Yaz played with graceful intensity in more games than any other American League player . . . In addition, he is the only A.L. player with over 3,000 hits and 400 home runs . . . Despite hitting over .300 just six times during his career, he managed to win three batting titles . . . One of only 11 players to ever win the Triple Crown . . . He is the last one to accomplish the "Hat Trick," batting .326 with 44 home runs and 121 RBI in 1967, the only season he was named the American League Most Valuable Player . . . Despite never reaching 200 hits in a season, he twice topped the league in hits while also leading the loop in doubles four times and runs scored three times . . . Won seven Gold Gloves . . . A perennial member of the American League All-Star team . . . Played in 18 mid-season classics, including 15 straight from 1965-79 . . . Played in two memorable World Series, batting .400 with three homers and five RBI in the 1967 Series against St. Louis and .310 in 1975 against Cincinnati . . . On September 12, 1979, Yaz singled against the New York Yankees for his 3,000th career hit . . . He was one of five to reach that plateau at the age of 40 or more.

Playing Career	AVG.	G	AB	R	H	2B	3B	HR	RBI	BB	SO	SB
23 Years	.285	3308	11988	1816	3419	646	59	452	1844	1845	1393	168

ROD CAREW

Born: October 1, 1945 — Gaton, Panama

Elected to Hall of Fame in 1991

Playing Career: Minnesota Twins (AL) 1967-78
California Angels (AL) 1979-85

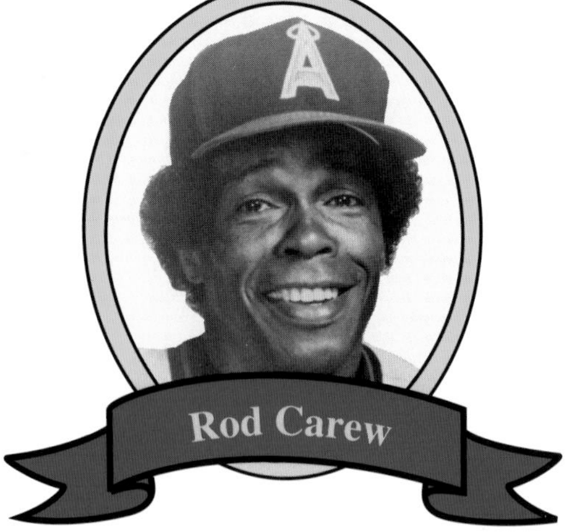
Rod Carew

A wizard with the bat, he lined, chopped and bunted his way to becoming the first player in nearly six seasons to reach the 3,000 hit plateau . . . He accomplished the feat on August 4, 1985 . . . Was named the American League Rookie of the Year in 1967 and 10 years later, earned his only A.L. Most Valuable Player honor after setting career highs with a .388 average, 239 hits, 16 triples and 128 runs scored . . . His seven batting titles—four consecutive—are surpassed only by Ty Cobb and Honus Wagner . . . He hit over .300 in 15 consecutive seasons from 1969-83 and missed the mark in two other seasons by less than 10 percentage points . . . Even though hitting was his trademark, Carew was one of the better base runners of his day . . . Despite stealing 353 bases, he never stole more than 49 in a season and never led the A.L. in that department . . . Another phenomenon involving this great hitter was that he never played in a World Series, although he played on a pair of Western Division Champions with the Minnesota Twins and California Angels . . . A fan favorite, he was voted to play in 17 All-Star Games, including 15 straight from 1967-81 . . . Traditionally the top vote-getter, he set an All-Star Game record when he received more than four million votes in 1977.

Playing Career	AVG.	G	AB	R	H	2B	3B	HR	RBI	BB	SO	SB
19 Years	.328	2469	9315	1424	3053	445	112	92	1015	1018	1028	353

©1992, Amoco Oil Company

Sale $
0000
Gallons
0000
Amoco
Ultimate
Lead-Free Premium

BACARDI
Ron Superior
JUST ADD
BACARDI
BACARDI
to Lemonade
Bacardi® rum. Made in Puerto Rico. BACARDI AND THE BAT DEVICE ARE REGISTERED TRADEMARKS OF BACARDI & COMPANY LIMITED. ©1992 BACARDI IMPORTS, INC., MIAMI, FL, 40% ALC. BY VOL.

ROBIN YOUNT

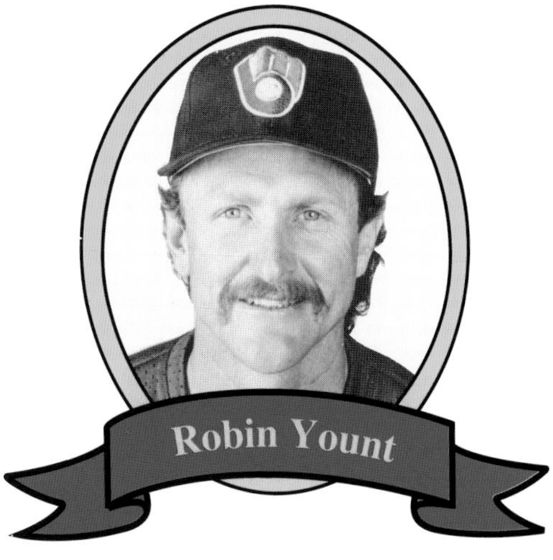
Robin Yount

Born: September 16, 1955 — Danville, Illinois

Playing Career: Milwaukee Brewers (AL) 1974-Present

The 17th player to collect 3,000 career hits . . . Accomplished the feat on September 9, 1992 against Cleveland's Jose Mesa at County Stadium . . . Yount singled to right-centerfield with one out in the seventh inning for the milestone hit . . .Yount becomes the third youngest player (36 years,11 months, 23 days) to reach that milestone . . . Ty Cobb and Henry Aaron were younger . . . Yount also becomes the first player to attain that landmark in seven seasons . . . Kansas City's George Brett will be the next player in line for 3,000 hits . . . The Brewers' all-time leader in nearly every offensive department, Yount is also among baseball's elite in many categories: With collecting his 3,000th career hit, Yount was 10th with 10,472 at bats; 12th with 550 doubles; 16th with 2,708 games played; 25th with 4,522 total bases; 29th with 2,085 singles; 32nd with 915 long hits; 36th with 1,560 runs scored; and 46th with 1,341 runs batted in. Yount also had 123 triples and 242 home runs . . . Yount is one of only 3 players to earn MVP honors at 2 different positions (Stan Musial and Hank Greenberg)—at shortstop in 1982 and centerfield in 1989 . . . Yount and Willie Mays are the only players to ever collect over 3,000 hits, 200 home runs, 200 stolen bases and 100 triples in a career . . . He is one of only 14 players to manage 200+ homers and stolen bases in his career . . . Yount was the youngest player in the league when he broke in as an 18-year old in 1974 . . . Two years later, he became the youngest to ever play in over 160 games . . . Was the first shortstop to lead the league in slugging (.578) and total bases (367) in the same season (1982) . . . He was the first shortstop to bat .300 with 20+ homers and 100+ RBI in the same season (1982) . . . Yount is one of only 3 players (Chuck Klein and Billy Herman) to collect 40+ doubles, 10+ triples, 20+ homers and 20+ stolen bases in the same season (1982) . . . Earned his only Gold Glove Award as a shortstop in 1982—the last by a Brewers player . . . The only player to ever have a pair of four-hit games in World Series history, ironically both came during the 1982 Classic . . . Although he played in only three All-Star Games, he was the Top Vote-getter in 1983 . . . Set a club record when he played in 276 consecutive games from August 13, 1987 to June 14, 1989 . . . Yount, who hit for the cycle on June 12, 1988, is one of only 7 players to do it and collect 3,000 hits (Tris Speaker, Honus Wagner, Stan Musial, Lou Brock, Carl Yastrzemski and Rod Carew are the others) . . . Following the 1989 season, Yount was named the American League "Player of the Decade" by *USA Today.*

Playing Career	AVG.	G	AB	R	H	2B	3B	HR	RBI	BB	SO	SB
19 Years	.286	2708	10472	1560	3000	550	123	242	1341	914	1251	257

ROBIN YOUNT vs THE AMERICAN LEAGUE
3,000 Hits/Career Intelligence Report

TOTALS	AVG.	AB	H	HR	RBI
Home	.290	5130	1489	123	691
Road	.283	5342	1511	119	650
Day	.287	3490	1002	93	464
Night	.286	6982	1998	149	877
vs Lefthanders	.285	2971	848	65	360
vs Righthanders	.287	7501	2152	177	981
Before The All-Star Game	.289	5653	1636	129	682
After The All-Star Game	.283	4819	1364	113	659
April	.290	1222	354	28	142
May	.293	1806	530	49	226
June	.283	1877	532	36	236
July	.294	1800	529	42	226
August	.273	1975	540	35	259
September-October	.287	1792	515	52	252
1970's	.270	3224	871	34	303
1980's	.305	5683	1731	174	821
1990's	.254	1565	398	34	217

TOTALS	AVG.	AB	H	HR	RBI
American League East	.287	5207	1493	120	718
American League West	.286	5265	1507	122	682
Baltimore Orioles	.277	849	235	21	114
Boston Red Sox	.275	901	248	19	92
California Angels	.281	797	224	12	94
Chicago White Sox	.286	765	219	24	110
Cleveland Indians	.286	906	259	18	104
Detroit Tigers	.277	928	257	20	110
Kansas City Royals	.302	734	222	18	92
Minnesota Twins	.263	756	199	18	90
New York Yankees	.281	875	246	19	115
Oakland Athletics	.282	753	212	16	100
Seattle Mariners	.286	700	200	23	106
Texas Rangers	.304	760	231	11	90
Toronto Blue Jays	.332	748	248	23	124

ROBIN
1974

"I probably need more experience and the best way of getting it is in the major leagues."

-Robin Yount, Opening Day, 1974

HIT	DATE	TYPE	PITCHER	OPPONENT
1	4-12-74	1B	Dave McNally	Baltimore
2	4-13-74	HR-1	Ross Grimsley	Baltimore
3	4-16-74	1B	Jim Perry	Cleveland
4	4-20-74	2B	Joe Coleman	at Detroit
5	4-21-74	1B	John Hiller	at Detroit
6	4-24-74	1B	Wilbur Wood	at Chicago
7	4-27-74	1B	Joe Decker	at Minnesota
8	4-27-74	1B	Joe Decker	at Minnesota
9	4-28-74	1B	Dick Woodson	at Minnesota
10	4-30-74	1B	Jim Bibby	Texas
11	5-01-74	1B	Steve Hargan	Texas
12	5-04-74	1B	Stan Bahsen	Chicago
13	5-07-74	1B	Joe Decker	Minnesota
14	5-07-74	1B	Joe Decker	Minnesota
15	5-11-74	1B	Doc Medich	at New York
16	5-12-74	1B	Mel Stottlemyre	at New York(1)
17	5-12-74	1B	Mel Stottlemyre	at New York(1)
18	5-13-74	1B	Doyle Alexander	at Baltimore
19	5-13-74	2B	Doyle Alexander	at Baltimore
20	5-14-74	2B	Jim Palmer	at Baltimore
21	5-14-74	1B	Don Hood	at Baltimore
22	5-17-74	1B	Doc Medich	New York
23	5-18-74	1B	Mel Stottlemyre	New York
24	5-19-74	1B	Pat Dobson	New York
25	5-25-74	1B	Reggie Cleveland	at Boston
26	5-26-74	1B	Bill Lee	at Boston
27	5-26-74	3B	Bill Lee	at Boston
28	5-27-74	1B	Nolan Ryan	at California
29	5-28-74	2B	Bill Stoneman	at California

HIT	DATE	TYPE	PITCHER	OPPONENT
30	5-28-74	1B	Skip Lockwood	at California
31	5-29-74	1B	Frank Tanana	at California
32	5-29-74	1B	Skip Lockwood	at California
33	5-31-74	3B	Rollie Fingers	at Oakland
34	6-02-74	1B	Jim Hunter	at Oakland
35	6-05-74	1B	Nolan Ryan	California
36	6-06-74	1B	Rudy May	California
37	6-08-74	1B	Dave Hamilton	Oakland
38	6-12-74	1B	Marty Pattin	at Kansas City
39	6-13-74	1B	Paul Splittorff	at Kansas City
40	6-13-74	1B	Paul Splittorff	at Kansas City
41	6-13-74	1B	Gene Garber	at Kansas City
42	6-14-74	1B	Jim Bibby	at Texas
43	6-16-74	1B	David Clyde	at Texas
44	6-16-74	3B	David Clyde	at Texas
45	6-22-74	HR-2	Ross Grimsley	Baltimore
46	6-23-74	2B	Dave McNally	Baltimore
47	6-24-74	1B	Luis Tiant	at Boston
48	6-26-74	1B	Bill Lee	at Boston
49	6-26-74	1B	Dick Pole	at Boston
50	6-27-74	1B	Joe Coleman	at Detroit
51	6-27-74	1B	Jim Ray	at Detroit
52	6-28-74	2B	Tom Walker	at Detroit
53	6-29-74	3B	Mickey Lolich	at Detroit
54	7-01-74	1B	Fritz Peterson	at Cleveland(2)
55	7-01-74	1B	Fritz Peterson	at Cleveland(2)
56	7-03-74	2B	Gaylord Perry	Cleveland
57	7-03-74	1B	Gaylord Perry	Cleveland
58	7-04-74	2B	Steve Arlin	Cleveland

HIT	DATE	TYPE	PITCHER	OPPONENT
59	7-04-74	1B	Bruce Ellingsen	Cleveland
60	7-04-74	1B	Milt Wilcox	Cleveland
61	7-05-74	HR-2	Dave Goltz	Minnesota(2)
62	7-06-74	1B	Joe Decker	Minnesota
63	7-07-74	1B	Ray Corbin	Minnesota(1)
64	7-08-74	1B	Jim Kaat	Chicago
65	7-09-74	1B	Skip Pitlock	Chicago
66	7-09-74	1B	Skip Pitlock	Chicago
67	7-09-74	2B	Rich Gossage	Chicago
68	7-10-74	1B	Wilbur Wood	Chicago
69	7-13-74	1B	Jim Bibby	Texas
70	7-13-74	3B	Jim Bibby	Texas
71	7-14-74	2B	Jackie Brown	Texas(1)
72	7-14-74	1B	Jackie Brown	Texas(1)
73	7-14-74	2B	Jackie Brown	Texas(1)
74	7-20-74	1B	Wilbur Wood	at Chicago
75	7-21-74	1B	Jim Kaat	at Chicago
76	7-26-74	1B	Pat Dobson	at New York
77	7-26-74	2B	Pat Dobson	at New York
78	7-27-74	2B	Wayne Garland	at Baltimore
79	7-31-74	1B	Sparky Lyle	New York
80	8-02-74	1B	Dave Lemanczyk	Detroit
81	8-04-74	2B	Dick Bosman	Cleveland(2)
82	8-08-74	1B	Luis Tiant	Boston
83	8-08-74	1B	Luis Tiant	Boston
84	8-09-74	1B	Steve Busby	at Kansas City
85	8-09-74	1B	Steve Busby	at Kansas City
86	8-12-74	1B	Steve Hargan	at Texas

M
19

YOUNT
1975

HIT	DATE	TYPE	PITCHER	OPPONENT
87	4-08-75	HR-1	Luis Tiant	at Boston
88	4-08-75	1B	Luis Tiant	at Boston
89	4-10-75	1B	Bill Lee	at Boston
90	4-10-75	1B	Bill Lee	at Boston
91	4-12-75	HR-1	Fritz Peterson	Cleveland
92	4-13-75	1B	Gaylord Perry	Cleveland
93	4-13-75	2B	Gaylord Perry	Cleveland
94	4-15-75	1B	Jim Palmer	at Baltimore
95	4-15-75	1B	Bob Reynolds	at Baltimore
96	4-18-75	2B	Gaylord Perry	at Cleveland
97	4-20-75	1B	Fritz Peterson	at Cleveland
98	4-20-75	1B	Fritz Peterson	at Cleveland
99	4-21-75	1B	Jim Palmer	Baltimore
100	4-23-75	1B	Mike Cuellar	Baltimore
101	4-25-75	2B	Pat Dobson	at New York
102	4-27-75	3B	Doc Medich	at New York(1)
103	4-27-75	1B	Doc Medich	at New York(1)
104	4-27-75	2B	Doc Medich	at New York(1)
105	4-27-75	HR-1	Jim Hunter	at New York(2)
106	4-30-75	1B	Dave Lemanczyk	Detroit
107	4-30-75	1B	Dave Lemanczyk	Detroit
108	4-30-75	1B	Dave Lemanczyk	Detroit
109	5-01-75	2B	Ray Bare	Detroit
110	5-01-75	HR-3	Tom Makowski	Detroit
111	5-02-75	2B	Doc Medich	New York
112	5-03-75	1B	Rudy May	New York
113	5-03-75	1B	Rudy May	New York
114	5-04-75	1B	Mike Wallace	New York
115	5-07-75	1B	Mickey Lolich	at Detroit
116	5-07-75	1B	Mickey Lolich	at Detroit
117	5-07-75	1B	Tom Walker	at Detroit
118	5-08-75	1B	John Hiller	at Detroit
119	5-24-75	1B	Jim Hughes	Minnesota
120	5-25-75	1B	Dave Goltz	Minnesota
121	5-27-75	1B	Wilbur Wood	Chicago
122	5-28-75	1B	Stan Bahnsen	Chicago
123	5-30-75	1B	Lindy McDaniel	Kansas City
124	6-01-75	2B	Steve Busby	Kansas City(1)
125	6-01-75	2B	Doug Bird	Kansas City(1)
126	6-01-75	1B	Al Fitzmorris	Kansas City(2)
127	6-02-75	1B	Vida Blue	at Oakland
128	6-02-75	1B	Vida Blue	at Oakland
129	6-04-75	1B	Ken Holtzman	at Oakland
130	6-04-75	2B	Ken Holtzman	at Oakland
131	6-06-75	1B	Frank Tanana	at California
132	6-08-75	2B	Claude Osteen	at Chicago
133	6-11-75	1B	Dick Bosman	Oakland
134	6-12-75	1B	Vida Blue	Oakland
135	6-13-75	1B	Bill Singer	California
136	6-13-75	1B	Dave Sells	California
137	6-14-75	1B	Nolan Ryan	California

HIT	DATE	TYPE	PITCHER	OPPONENT
138	6-15-75	2B	Frank Tanana	California(1)
139	6-15-75	2B	Frank Tanana	California(1)
140	6-15-75	1B	Frank Tanana	California(1)
141	6-15-75	1B	Andy Hassler	California(2)
142	6-15-75	1B	Andy Hassler	California(2)
143	6-15-75	1B	Andy Hassler	California(2)
144	6-16-75	1B	Rudy May	at New York
145	6-16-75	1B	Rudy May	at New York
146	6-18-75	1B	Doc Medich	at New York
147	6-18-75	1B	Doc Medich	at New York
148	6-20-75	1B	Roric Harrison	at Cleveland
149	6-20-75	1B	Don Hood	at Cleveland
150	6-21-75	1B	Tom Buskey	at Cleveland
151	6-22-75	1B	Jim Bibby	at Cleveland
152	6-23-75	1B	Joe Coleman	Detroit
153	6-24-75	1B	Ray Bare	Detroit(1)
154	6-24-75	2B	Ray Bare	Detroit(1)
155	6-24-75	1B	Lerrin LaGrow	Detroit(2)
156	6-27-75	1B	Jim Bibby	Cleveland
157	6-28-75	2B	Eric Raich	Cleveland
158	6-28-75	1B	Jackie Brown	Cleveland
159	7-01-75	1B	Pat Dobson	New York
160	7-02-75	1B	Bill Lee	Boston(2)
161	7-03-75	2B	Roger Moret	Boston
162	7-04-75	1B	Ray Bare	at Detroit
163	7-06-75	1B	Mickey Lolich	at Detroit(1)
164	7-06-75	1B	Mickey Lolich	at Detroit(1)
165	7-08-75	1B	Dennis Leonard	at Kansas City
166	7-08-75	1B	Dennis Leonard	at Kansas City
167	7-09-75	1B	Nelson Briles	at Kansas City
168	7-09-75	1B	Paul Splittorff	at Kansas City
169	7-11-75	1B	Claude Osteen	Chicago
170	7-12-75	1B	Jim Kaat	Chicago
171	7-12-75	1B	Cecil Upshaw	Chicago
172	7-21-75	1B	Claude Osteen	at Chicago
173	7-21-75	1B	Cecil Upshaw	at Chicago
174	7-21-75	1B	Dave Hamilton	at Chicago
175	7-22-75	2B	Steve Busby	Kansas City(1)
176	7-22-75	1B	Al Fitzmorris	Kansas City(2)
177	7-23-75	1B	Marty Pattin	Kansas City
178	7-25-75	1B	Mike Torrez	Baltimore
179	7-27-75	1B	Jim Palmer	Baltimore(1)
180	7-27-75	HR-2	Paul Mitchell	Baltimore(2)
181	7-28-75	1B	Rick Wise	at Boston
182	7-28-75	1B	Rick Wise	at Boston
183	7-29-75	1B	Diego Segui	at Boston
184	7-30-75	2B	Reggie Cleveland	at Boston
185	8-01-75	1B	Jim Palmer	at Baltimore(1)
186	8-02-75	1B	Mike Torrez	at Baltimore

HIT	DATE	TYPE	PITCHER	OPPONENT
187	8-03-75	1B	Mike Cuellar	at Baltimore
188	8-04-75	1B	Rudy May	New York
189	8-05-75	1B	Jim Hunter	New York
190	8-09-75	1B	Ferguson Jenkins	Texas
191	8-10-75	1B	Bill Hands	Texas
192	8-12-75	2B	Jim Hughes	at Minnesota
193	8-12-75	2B	Mark Wiley	at Minnesota
194	8-13-75	1B	Dave Goltz	at Minnesota
195	8-13-75	2B	Dave Goltz	at Minnesota
196	8-14-75	1B	Glenn Abbott	at Oakland
197	8-16-75	1B	Stan Bahnsen	at Oakland
198	8-17-75	1B	Bill Singer	at California
199	8-18-75	2B	Frank Tanana	at California
200	8-19-75	2B	Andy Hassler	at California
201	8-23-75	1B	Glenn Abbott	Oakland(1)
202	8-23-75	2B	Stan Bahnsen	Oakland(2)
203	8-24-75	HR-1	Rollie Fingers	Oakland
204	8-28-75	1B	Tommy Moore	Texas
205	8-28-75	1B	Tommy Moore	Texas
206	8-29-75	1B	Jim Umbarger	Texas
207	8-31-75	HR-2	Gaylord Perry	Texas
208	9-01-75	2B	Vern Ruhle	at Detroit
209	9-01-75	1B	Dave Lemanczyk	at Detroit
210	9-03-75	1B	Fritz Peterson	Cleveland
211	9-03-75	1B	Bob Reynolds	Cleveland
212	9-05-75	1B	Bill Lee	Boston
213	9-07-75	1B	Reggie Cleveland	Boston(1)
214	9-07-75	1B	Reggie Cleveland	Boston(1)
215	9-07-75	2B	Jim Willoughby	Boston(2)
216	9-11-75	1B	Jim Hunter	at New York
217	9-11-75	1B	Jim Hunter	at New York
218	9-13-75	1B	Dick Drago	at Boston
219	9-13-75	2B	Dick Drago	at Boston
220	9-13-75	2B	Reggie Cleveland	at Boston
221	9-13-75	1B	Reggie Cleveland	at Boston
222	9-14-75	1B	Bill Lee	at Boston
223	9-15-75	HR-1	Roger Moret	at Boston
224	9-16-75	1B	Larry Gura	New York
225	9-17-75	3B	Doc Medich	New York
226	9-17-75	1B	Tippy Martinez	New York
227	9-19-75	1B	Doyle Alexander	at Baltimore
228	9-20-75	1B	Jim Palmer	at Baltimore
229	9-22-75	2B	Jim Strickland	at Cleveland
230	9-23-75	1B	Dave LaRoche	at Cleveland
231	9-24-75	1B	Fritz Peterson	at Cleveland
232	9-24-75	1B	Jackie Brown	at Cleveland
233	9-26-75	1B	Ray Bare	Detroit
234	9-26-75	1B	Ray Bare	Detroit
235	9-28-75	1B	Dave Lemanczyk	Detroit

"I admit I'm anxious to get going. I just want to get into the uniform and go through the routine again." — *Robin Yount, 1975*

BREWE

ROBIN
M
1976

HIT	DATE	TYPE	PITCHER	OPPONENT
236	4-10-76	1B	Ed Figueroa	New York
237	4-10-76	1B	Ed Figueroa	New York
238	4-10-76	1B	Sparky Lyle	New York
239	4-13-76	1B	John Hiller	at Detroit
240	4-16-76	1B	Jim Umbarger	at Texas
241	4-18-76	1B	Nelson Briles	at Texas
242	4-18-76	1B	Nelson Briles	at Texas
243	4-20-76	1B	Dennis Leonard	Kansas City
244	4-20-76	1B	Dennis Leonard	Kansas City
245	4-22-76	1B	Al Fitzmorris	Kansas City
246	4-26-76	1B	Frank Tanana	California
247	4-28-76	2B	Wilbur Wood	at Chicago
248	4-29-76	1B	Rich Gossage	at Chicago
249	4-29-76	1B	Clay Carroll	at Chicago
250	5-01-76	1B	Bill Campbell	at Minnesota
251	5-01-76	2B	Bill Campbell	at Minnesota
252	5-07-76	1B	Jim Hughes	Minnesota
253	5-07-76	1B	Steve Luebber	Minnesota
254	5-09-76	1B	Dave Goltz	Minnesota
255	5-09-76	1B	Dave Goltz	Minnesota
256	5-12-76	1B	Ken Holtzman	Baltimore
257	5-13-76	1B	Jim Palmer	Baltimore
258	5-14-76	1B	Dick Pole	at Boston
259	5-16-76	1B	Rick Wise	at Boston
260	5-16-76	1B	Rick Wise	at Boston
261	5-17-76	1B	Jim Palmer	at Baltimore
262	5-17-76	1B	Jim Palmer	at Baltimore
263	5-19-76	1B	Mike Cuellar	at Baltimore
264	5-19-76	1B	Mike Cuellar	at Baltimore
265	5-19-76	1B	Wayne Garland	at Baltimore
266	5-21-76	1B	Pat Dobson	at Cleveland
267	5-23-76	1B	Jackie Brown	at Cleveland(1)
268	5-23-76	2B	Fritz Peterson	at Cleveland(2)
269	5-23-76	1B	Jim Kern	at Cleveland(2)
270	5-26-76	1B	Dick Pole	Boston
271	5-29-76	1B	Jackie Brown	Cleveland
272	5-29-76	1B	Jackie Brown	Cleveland
273	5-31-76	1B	Mark Fidrych	at Detroit
274	5-31-76	1B	Mark Fidrych	at Detroit
275	6-01-76	1B	Ray Bare	at Detroit(1)
276	6-01-76	1B	Steve Grilli	at Detroit(1)
277	6-02-76	1B	Vern Ruhle	at Detroit
278	6-02-76	3B	Vern Ruhle	at Detroit
279	6-02-76	1B	Vern Ruhle	at Detroit
280	6-02-76	1B	Vern Ruhle	at Detroit
281	6-05-76	1B	Al Fitzmorris	at K. C.(1)
282	6-05-76	1B	Al Fitzmorris	at K. C.(1)
283	6-05-76	1B	Paul Splittorff	at K. C.(2)
284	6-06-76	3B	Doug Bird	at Kansas City
285	6-06-76	1B	Doug Bird	at Kansas City
286	6-06-76	1B	Doug Bird	at Kansas City
287	6-06-76	1B	Steve Mingori	at Kansas City
288	6-08-76	2B	Bart Johnson	Chicago
289	6-08-76	1B	Bart Johnson	Chicago

HIT	DATE	TYPE	PITCHER	OPPONENT
290	6-08-76	1B	Bart Johnson	Chicago
291	6-12-76	1B	Paul Mitchell	Oakland
292	6-12-76	1B	Rollie Fingers	Oakland
293	6-13-76	1B	Mike Torrez	Oakland
294	6-13-76	1B	Dick Bosman	Oakland
295	6-18-76	3B	Dick Bosman	at Oakland
296	6-19-76	1B	Glenn Abbott	at Oakland(1)
297	6-19-76	1B	Mike Torrez	at Oakland(2)
298	6-19-76	2B	Mike Torrez	at Oakland(2)
299	6-19-76	2B	Stan Bahnsen	at Oakland(2)
300	6-19-76	HR-1	Stan Bahnsen	at Oakland(2)
301	6-21-76	1B	John Hiller	Detroit
302	6-22-76	2B	Dave Roberts	Detroit
303	6-23-76	1B	Jim Crawford	Detroit
304	6-23-76	1B	Jim Crawford	Detroit
305	6-25-76	1B	Dock Ellis	at New York
306	6-27-76	2B	Jim Hunter	at New York
307	7-01-76	1B	Ferguson Jenkins	Boston
308	7-01-76	1B	Tom Murphy	Boston
309	7-03-76	2B	Rick Jones	Boston
310	7-04-76	1B	Rick Wise	Boston
311	7-05-76	1B	Eddie Bane	Minnesota
312	7-05-76	1B	Eddie Bane	Minnesota
313	7-06-76	1B	Jim Hughes	Minnesota
314	7-06-76	HR-2	Jim Hughes	Minnesota
315	7-08-76	1B	Nelson Briles	Texas
316	7-08-76	1B	Nelson Briles	Texas
317	7-09-76	1B	Steve Hargan	Texas
318	7-10-76	1B	Gaylord Perry	Texas
319	7-11-76	1B	Bert Blyleven	Texas(1)
320	7-11-76	1B	Steve Barr	Texas(2)
321	7-11-76	1B	Jeff Terpko	Texas(2)
322	7-15-76	1B	Ken Brett	at Chicago
323	7-16-76	1B	Bart Johnson	at Chicago
324	7-16-76	1B	Dave Hamilton	at Chicago
325	7-17-76	1B	John Odom	at Chicago
326	7-18-76	1B	Francisco Barrios	at Chicago
327	7-19-76	1B	Paul Hartzell	California(1)
328	7-19-76	1B	Paul Hartzell	California(1)
329	7-19-76	1B	Don Kirkwood	California(2)
330	7-19-76	1B	Don Kirwood	California(2)
331	7-20-76	1B	Dick Drago	California
332	7-21-76	2B	Al Fitzmorris	at Kansas City
333	7-21-76	1B	Al Fitzmorris	at Kansas City
334	7-22-76	1B	Paul Splittorff	Kansas City
335	7-23-76	1B	Jim Palmer	at Balitmore
336	7-24-76	1B	Mike Cuellar	at Baltimore(1)
337	7-24-76	1B	Fred Holdsworth	at Baltimore(1)
338	7-25-76	1B	Fred Holdsworth	at Baltimore
339	7-28-76	1B	Dave Roberts	at Detroit
340	7-30-76	1B	Dennis Eckersley	Cleveland
341	7-31-76	1B	Jim Bibby	Cleveland
342	8-02-76	1B	Rudy May	Baltimore
343	8-03-76	1B	Ross Grimsley	Baltimore

HIT	DATE	TYPE	PITCHER	OPPONENT
344	8-04-76	2B	Jim Hunter	New York(1)
345	8-04-76	1B	Ken Holtman	New York(2)
346	8-05-76	1B	Dock Ellis	New York
347	8-07-76	1B	Luis Tiant	at Boston
348	8-11-76	2B	Mike Torrez	at Oakland
349	8-12-76	1B	Rollie Fingers	at Oakland
350	8-14-76	2B	Don Kirkwood	at California
351	8-15-76	1B	Gary Ross	at California
352	8-15-76	1B	Gary Ross	at California
353	8-16-76	1B	Dick Bosman	Oakland
354	8-16-76	1B	Dick Bosman	Oakland
355	8-17-76	1B	Mike Norris	Oakland
356	8-17-76	1B	Paul Lindblad	Oakland
357	8-19-76	1B	Steve Mingori	Kansas City
358	8-21-76	1B	Marty Pattin	Kansas City
359	8-22-76	2B	Doug Bird	Kansas City
360	8-23-76	1B	Jim Umbarger	at Texas
361	8-23-76	1B	Jeff Terpko	at Texas
362	8-24-76	1B	Nelson Briles	at Texas
363	8-24-76	1B	Steve Foucault	at Texas
364	8-25-76	1B	Joe Hoerner	at Texas
365	8-27-76	1B	Ken Kravec	Chicago
366	8-27-76	1B	Ken Kravec	Chicago
367	8-31-76	1B	Jim Hughes	at Minnesota(2)
368	9-01-76	1B	Bill Singer	at Minnesota
369	9-02-76	2B	Eddie Bane	at Minnesota
370	9-03-76	1B	Bill Laxton	at Detroit
371	9-03-76	1B	Steve Grilli	at Detroit
372	9-06-76	1B	Stan Thomas	Cleveland(1)
373	9-06-76	2B	Jim Bibby	Cleveland(2)
374	9-07-76	1B	Jackie Brown	Cleveland
375	9-07-76	1B	Don Hood	Cleveland
376	9-09-76	1B	Ken Holtzman	at New York
377	9-10-76	1B	Jim Hunter	at New York
378	9-11-76	1B	Wayne Garland	Baltimore(1)
379	9-11-76	1B	Mike Flanagan	Baltimore(2)
380	9-11-76	2B	Mike Flanagan	Baltimore(2)
381	9-11-76	1B	Mike Flanagan	Baltimore(2)
382	9-14-76	1B	Rick Wise	Boston
383	9-14-76	1B	Jim Willoughby	Boston
384	9-16-76	1B	Rick Kreuger	Boston
385	9-19-76	1B	Jim Hunter	New York
386	9-21-76	1B	Luis Tiant	at Boston(1)
387	9-23-76	2B	Bill Lee	at Boston
388	9-23-76	1B	Bill Lee	at Boston
389	9-23-76	2B	Bill Lee	at Boston
390	9-24-76	1B	Dennis Eckersley	at Cleveland
391	9-25-76	1B	Pat Dobson	at Cleveland
392	9-28-76	1B	Wayne Garland	at Baltimore(1)
393	9-28-76	1B	Wayne Garland	at Baltimore(1)
394	9-29-76	1B	Scott McGregor	at Baltimore
395	9-29-76	1B	Scott McGregor	at Baltimore
396	10-2-76	1B	Mark Fidrych	Detroit

"I've made some transitions, but I never place personal goals ahead of the team."
— Robin Yount, 1976

YOUNT
1977

HIT	DATE	TYPE	PITCHER	OPPONENT
397	4-09-77	1B	Ed Figueroa	at New York
398	4-09-77	1B	Ed Figueroa	at New York
399	4-10-77	1B	Don Gullett	at New York
400	4-14-77	1B	Rudy May	Baltimore
401	4-14-77	1B	Rudy May	Baltimore
402	4-16-77	1B	Ken Holtzman	New York
403	4-16-77	1B	Ken Holtzman	New York
404	4-17-77	1B	Dock Ellis	New York
405	4-17-77	HR-1	Dock Ellis	New York
406	4-20-77	1B	Mike Torrez	at Oakland
407	4-20-77	1B	Mike Torrez	at Oakland
408	4-22-77	1B	Wayne Simpson	at California
409	4-22-77	1B	Dick Drago	at California
410	4-23-77	1B	Paul Hartzell	at California
411	4-24-77	1B	Frank Tanana	at California
412	4-24-77	1B	Don Kirkwood	at California
413	4-26-77	1B	Rick Wise	Boston
414	4-27-77	1B	Reggie Cleveland	Boston
415	4-29-77	1B	Pat Dobson	Cleveland
416	4-30-77	1B	Dennis Eckersley	Cleveland
417	5-01-77	HR-3	Wayne Garland	Cleveland(1)
418	5-01-77	2B	Wayne Garland	Cleveland(1)
419	5-01-77	1B	Jim Bibby	Cleveland(2)
420	5-01-77	2B	Jim Bibby	Cleveland(2)
421	5-02-77	1B	Jerry Johnson	at Toronto
422	5-04-77	2B	Bill Singer	at Toronto
423	5-05-77	1B	Jerry Garvin	at Toronto
424	5-06-77	1B	Dave Roberts	at Detroit
425	5-07-77	1B	Dave Rozema	at Detroit
426	5-08-77	2B	Vern Ruhle	at Detroit
427	5-08-77	1B	Vern Ruhle	at Detroit
428	5-08-77	1B	Fernando Arroyo	at Detroit
429	5-15-77	2B	Steve Foucault	Detroit(1)
430	5-15-77	2B	Dave Roberts	Detroit(2)
431	5-17-77	1B	Jerry Johnson	Toronto
432	5-18-77	1B	Dave Lemanczyk	Toronto
433	5-18-77	1B	Dave Lemanczyk	Toronto
434	5-18-77	1B	Pete Vuckovich	Toronto
435	5-19-77	1B	Jerry Johnson	Toronto
436	5-20-77	2B	Tom House	at Boston
437	5-20-77	1B	Tom Murphy	at Boston
438	5-21-77	1B	Bob Stanley	at Boston
439	5-22-77	1B	Reggie Cleveland	at Boston(1)
440	5-22-77	1B	Ferguson Jenkins	at Boston(2)
441	5-22-77	1B	Tom House	at Boston(2)
442	5-23-77	1B	Dyar Miller	at Baltimore
443	5-25-77	2B	Bart Johnson	Chicago
444	5-27-77	1B	Doyle Alexander	Texas
445	5-28-77	1B	Nelson Briles	Texas
446	5-28-77	1B	Nelson Briles	Texas
447	5-29-77	1B	Mike Marshall	Texas
448	5-29-77	1B	Mike Marshall	Texas
449	5-29-77	2B	Steve Hargan	Texas
450	5-29-77	1B	Adrian Devine	Texas
451	5-30-77	1B	Chris Knapp	at Chicago(1)
452	5-30-77	1B	Bart Johnson	at Chicago(1)
453	5-30-77	1B	Steve Stone	at Chicago(2)
454	5-30-77	1B	Steve Stone	at Chicago(2)
455	5-30-77	1B	Steve Stone	at Chicago(2)
456	6-03-77	1B	Mike Marshall	at Texas
457	6-03-77	2B	Mike Marshall	at Texas
458	6-03-77	1B	Steve Hargan	at Texas
459	6-03-77	1B	Steve Hargan	at Texas
460	6-04-77	1B	Bert Blyleven	at Texas
461	6-04-77	2B	Gaylord Perry	at Texas
462	6-06-77	1B	Rudy May	Baltimore
463	6-07-77	1B	Ross Grimsley	Baltimore
464	6-07-77	2B	Ross Grimsley	Baltimore
465	6-08-77	1B	Mike Torrez	New York
466	6-09-77	1B	Don Gullett	New York
467	6-09-77	1B	Don Gullett	New York
468	6-10-77	1B	Doug Bird	Kansas City
469	6-10-77	2B	Doug Bird	Kansas City
470	6-12-77	1B	Jim Colborn	Kansas City
471	6-12-77	1B	Jim Colborn	Kansas City
472	6-15-77	2B	Mike Flanagan	at Baltimore
473	6-15-77	1B	Scott McGregor	at Baltimore
474	6-16-77	1B	Rudy May	at Baltimore
475	6-16-77	2B	Rudy May	at Baltimore
476	6-18-77	1B	Gary Nolan	California
477	6-19-77	1B	Frank Tanana	California
478	6-21-77	1B	Doug Bair	Oakland
479	6-22-77	1B	Vida Blue	Oakland
480	6-22-77	2B	Vida Blue	Oakland
481	6-24-77	1B	John Montague	Seattle
482	6-24-77	1B	Tom House	Seattle
483	6-26-77	1B	Glenn Abbott	Seattle
484	6-26-77	1B	Glenn Abbott	Seattle
485	6-27-77	1B	Dave Goltz	at Minnesota
486	6-27-77	1B	Dave Goltz	at Minnesota
487	6-29-77	1B	Dave Johnson	at Minnesota
488	7-02-77	1B	Glenn Abbott	at Seattle
489	7-02-77	2B	Glenn Abbott	at Seattle
490	7-02-77	1B	Glenn Abbott	at Seattle
491	7-03-77	2B	Dick Pole	at Seattle
492	7-06-77	1B	Andy Hassler	at Kansas City
493	7-06-77	1B	Andy Hassler	at Kansas City
494	7-06-77	2B	Marty Pattin	at Kansas City
495	7-08-77	1B	Reggie Cleveland	Boston
496	7-09-77	2B	Ferguson Jenkins	Boston
497	7-09-77	1B	Ferguson Jenkins	Boston
498	7-09-77	1B	Ferguson Jenkins	Boston
499	7-10-77	1B	Luis Tiant	Boston(1)
500	7-10-77	1B	Luis Tiant	Boston(1)
501	7-13-77	3B	Jim Hunter	New York
502	7-14-77	1B	Ed Figueroa	New York
503	7-15-77	1B	Mike Flanagan	Baltimore
504	7-24-77	1B	Rudy May	at Baltimore
505	7-26-77	1B	Don Aase	at Boston
506	7-26-77	2B	Don Aase	at Boston
507	7-26-77	2B	Don Aase	at Boston
508	7-27-77	2B	Rick Wise	at Boston
509	7-27-77	1B	Rick Wise	at Boston
510	7-29-77	1B	Tom Murphy	at Toronto
511	7-30-77	1B	Jeff Byrd	at Toronto
512	7-30-77	1B	Pete Vuckovich	at Toronto
513	8-02-77	1B	Dennis Eckersley	Cleveland(1)
514	8-02-77	1B	Dennis Eckersley	Cleveland(1)
515	8-02-77	1B	Wayne Garland	Cleveland(2)
516	8-02-77	1B	Wayne Garland	Cleveland(2)
517	8-03-77	1B	Jim Bibby	Cleveland
518	8-03-77	1B	Pat Dobson	Cleveland
519	8-05-77	1B	Jeff Byrd	Toronto
520	8-05-77	1B	Pete Vuckovich	Toronto
521	8-06-77	1B	Dave Lemanczyk	Toronto
522	8-06-77	2B	Dave Lemanczyk	Toronto
523	8-06-77	1B	Dave Lemanczyk	Toronto
524	8-07-77	1B	Jerry Garvin	Toronto(1)
525	8-07-77	1B	Tom Murphy	Toronto(1)
526	8-07-77	3B	Jim Clancy	Toronto(2)
527	8-08-77	1B	Jim Crawford	at Detroit
528	8-08-77	1B	Jim Crawford	at Detroit
529	8-08-77	1B	Jim Crawford	at Detroit
530	8-09-77	1B	John Hiller	at Detroit(2)
531	8-12-77	1B	Jim Kern	at Cleveland
532	8-13-77	1B	Jim Bibby	at Cleveland
533	8-13-77	1B	Jim Bibby	at Cleveland
534	8-14-77	2B	Wayne Garland	at Cleveland(1)
535	8-14-77	1B	Al Fitzmorris	at Cleveland(2)
536	8-14-77	1B	Pat Dobson	at Cleveland(2)
537	8-16-77	1B	Doyle Alexander	Texas
538	8-17-77	2B	Rick Wise	Boston
539	8-18-77	1B	Ferguson Jenkins	Boston
540	8-18-77	1B	Ferguson Jenkins	Boston
541	8-20-77	1B	Steve Stone	Chicago
542	8-21-77	1B	Lerrin LaGrow	Chicago(2)
543	8-22-77	1B	Adrian Devine	at Texas
544	8-23-77	1B	Dock Ellis	at Texas
545	8-27-77	3B	Francisco Barrios	at Chicago
546	8-28-77	1B	Wilbur Wood	at Chicago
547	8-28-77	2B	Bart Johnson	at Chicago
548	8-28-77	2B	Don Kirkwood	at Chicago
549	8-30-77	3B	Dave Rozema	Detroit
550	8-30-77	2B	Dave Rozema	Detroit
551	8-30-77	1B	Dave Rozema	Detroit
552	8-31-77	1B	Milt Wilcox	Detroit
553	9-02-77	1B	Andy Hassler	at K. C.(1)
554	9-04-77	1B	Marty Pattin	at Kansas City
555	9-05-77	2B	Frank Tanana	at California
556	9-07-77	2B	Paul Hartzell	at California
557	9-11-77	2B	Vida Blue	at Oakland
558	9-11-77	2B	Vida Blue	at Oakland
559	9-13-77	HR-3	Glenn Abbott	at Seattle
560	9-14-77	HR-2	John Montague	at Seattle
561	9-16-77	1B	Joe Coleman	Oakland
562	9-17-77	1B	Craig Mitchell	Oakland
563	9-18-77	1B	Matt Keough	Oakland
564	9-20-77	2B	John Montague	Seattle
565	9-21-77	1B	Doc Medich	Seattle
566	9-21-77	1B	Doc Medich	Seattle
567	9-25-77	1B	Paul Thormodsgard	at Minnesota(1)
568	9-25-77	1B	Gary Serum	at Minnesota(1)
569	9-27-77	1B	Paul Hartzell	California
570	10-1-77	1B	Pete Redfern	Minnesota

"I'm tired of losing. The most important thing is being able to enjoy baseball."
— Robin Yount, 1977

ROBIN
1978

HIT	DATE	TYPE	PITCHER	OPPONENT
571	5-07-78	1B	Steve Mingori	Kansas City
572	5-16-78	1B	Doyle Alexander	at Texas
573	5-17-78	1B	Jack Billingham	Detroit
574	5-17-78	3B	Jack Billingham	Detroit
575	5-17-78	1B	Jack Billingham	Detroit
576	5-18-78	1B	Jack Morris	Detroit
577	5-18-78	1B	Fernando Arroyo	Detroit
578	5-19-78	1B	Frank Tanana	California
579	5-20-78	1B	Ken Brett	California
580	5-20-78	1B	Dyar Miller	California
581	5-24-78	1B	Rick Langford	at Oakland
582	5-26-78	1B	Ken Brett	at California
583	5-27-78	1B	Tom Griffin	at California
584	5-27-78	1B	Dyar Miller	at California
585	5-28-78	1B	Paul Hartzell	at California
586	5-29-78	1B	Pete Broberg	Oakland
587	5-30-78	2B	Dave Heaverlo	Oakland
588	5-30-78	1B	Bob Lacey	Oakland
589	6-03-78	1B	Mike Paxton	Cleveland
590	6-04-78	1B	Dennis Kinney	Cleveland
591	6-06-78	1B	Milt Wilcox	Detroit
592	6-07-78	1B	Jim Slaton	Detroit
593	6-10-78	1B	Jerry Garvin	Toronto
594	6-11-78	2B	Tom Underwood	Toronto(1)
595	6-11-78	HR-1	Tom Murphy	Toronto(2)
596	6-12-78	1B	Milt Wilcox	at Detroit
597	6-12-78	1B	Jack Morris	at Detroit
598	6-13-78	1B	Jim Slaton	at Detroit
599	6-13-78	1B	Steve Foucault	at Detroit
600	6-14-78	1B	Don Kirkwood	at Toronto(1)
601	6-14-78	2B	Tom Murphy	at Toronto(1)
602	6-14-78	1B	Jerry Garvin	at Toronto(2)
603	6-14-78	1B	Jerry Garvin	at Toronto(2)
604	6-16-78	1B	Rick Wise	at Cleveland
605	6-16-78	1B	Rick Wise	at Cleveland
606	6-18-78	1B	Rick Waits	at Cleveland(1)
607	6-20-78	1B	Don Stanhouse	Baltimore
608	6-21-78	2B	Dennis Martinez	Baltimore
609	6-22-78	1B	Mike Flanagan	Baltimore
610	6-25-78	1B	Mike Parrott	Seattle
611	6-27-78	2B	Dave Goltz	Minnesota
612	6-27-78	1B	Mike Marshall	Minnesota
613	6-28-78	1B	Dick Tidrow	New York(1)
614	6-28-78	1B	Larry McCall	New York(2)
615	6-30-78	1B	Mike Parrott	at Seattle
616	6-30-78	2B	Tom House	at Seattle
617	7-01-78	1B	Paul Mitchell	at Seattle
618	7-02-78	1B	Dick Pole	at Seattle
619	7-03-78	1B	Roger Erickson	at Minnesota

HIT	DATE	TYPE	PITCHER	OPPONENT
620	7-04-78	2B	Gary Serum	at Minnesota
621	7-05-78	1B	Dave Goltz	at Minnesota
622	7-05-78	1B	Dave Goltz	at Minnesota
623	7-07-78	3B	Ron Guidry	New York
624	7-08-78	1B	Dave Rajsich	New York
625	7-08-78	1B	Dave Rajsich	New York
626	7-08-78	1B	Rich Gossage	New York
627	7-09-78	2B	Don Gullett	New York
628	7-13-78	3B	Paul Splittorff	Kansas City
629	7-13-78	1B	Randy McGilberry	Kansas City
630	7-14-78	2B	Rich Gale	Kansas City
631	7-14-78	1B	Rich Gale	Kansas City
632	7-16-78	3B	Steve Stone	Baltimore
633	7-16-78	1B	Steve Stone	Baltimore
634	7-17-78	3B	Francisco Barrios	Chicago
635	7-17-78	1B	Jim Willoughby	Chicago
636	7-19-78	1B	Mike Torrez	Boston
637	7-21-78	1B	Doc Medich	at Texas
638	7-22-78	2B	Jon Matlack	at Texas
639	7-23-78	1B	Steve Comer	at Texas
640	7-23-78	1B	Paul Lindblad	at Texas
641	7-25-78	1B	Francisco Barrios	at Texas
642	7-26-78	HR-2	Frank Tanana	California
643	7-27-78	1B	Nolan Ryan	California
644	7-27-78	1B	Nolan Ryan	California
645	7-27-78	1B	Al Fitzmorris	California
646	7-28-78	1B	Jesse Jefferson	at Toronto
647	7-29-78	1B	Dave Lemanczyk	at Toronto
648	7-29-78	1B	Dave Lemanczyk	at Toronto
649	7-29-78	1B	Dave Lemanczyk	at Toronto
650	7-30-78	3B	Tom Murphy	at Toronto
651	8-01-78	1B	Jim Palmer	at Baltimore
652	8-04-78	1B	Jim Wright	Boston
653	8-04-78	2B	Jim Wright	Boston
654	8-05-78	1B	Dennis Eckersley	Boston
655	8-06-78	1B	Luis Tiant	Boston
656	8-09-78	1B	Ed Figueroa	at New York
657	8-09-78	1B	Ken Clay	at New York
658	8-09-78	3B	Larry McCall	at New York
659	8-10-78	2B	Ron Guidry	at New York
660	8-10-78	1B	Ron Guidry	at New York
661	8-11-78	1B	Luis Tiant	at Boston
662	8-11-78	1B	Luis Tiant	at Boston
663	8-12-78	1B	Bill Campbell	at Boston(2)
664	8-13-78	1B	Mike Torrez	at Boston
665	8-15-78	1B	Dave Lemanczyk	Toronto
666	8-15-78	1B	Dave Lemanczyk	Toronto
667	8-15-78	2B	Joe Coleman	Toronto
668	8-16-78	1B	Jesse Jefferson	Toronto

HIT	DATE	TYPE	PITCHER	OPPONENT
669	8-16-78	HR-2	Jesse Jefferson	Toronto(1)
670	8-16-78	1B	Balor Moore	Toronto
671	8-17-78	2B	Mike Willis	Toronto
672	8-17-78	1B	Mike Willis	Toronto
673	8-18-78	1B	Dave Rozema	Detroit
674	8-19-78	2B	Milt Wilcox	Detroit
675	8-20-78	1B	Kip Young	Detroit
676	8-22-78	3B	David Clyde	Cleveland
677	8-24-78	1B	Mike Paxton	Cleveland
678	8-24-78	2B	Mike Paxton	Cleveland
679	8-25-78	1B	Kip Young	at Detroit
680	8-26-78	1B	Jack Billingham	at Detroit
681	8-26-78	1B	Dave Tobik	at Detroit
682	8-26-78	1B	Dave Tobik	at Detroit
683	8-27-78	1B	John Hiller	at Detroit
684	8-28-78	HR-3	Dave Rozema	at Detroit
685	8-31-78	1B	Rick Waits	at Cleveland(2)
686	8-31-78	2B	Rick Waits	at Cleveland(2)
687	9-01-78	1B	Ferguson Jenkins	Texas
688	9-02-78	1B	Doc Medich	Texas
689	9-03-78	1B	Jon Matlack	Texas
690	9-04-78	3B	Glenn Abbott	Seattle(1)
691	9-04-78	1B	Glenn Abbott	Seattle(1)
692	9-04-78	1B	Bryon McLaughlin	Seattle(1)
693	9-04-78	1B	Mike Parrott	Seattle(2)
694	9-06-78	2B	Jesse Jefferson	at Toronto
695	9-06-78	HR-2	Jesse Jefferson	at Toronto
696	9-06-78	1B	Jesse Jefferson	at Toronto
697	9-06-78	HR-2	Jesse Jefferson	at Toronto
698	9-07-78	1B	Jim Clancy	at Toronto
699	9-07-78	1B	Jim Clancy	at Toronto
700	9-08-78	2B	Gary Serum	at Minnesota
701	9-11-78	1B	Byron McLaughlin	at Seattle
702	9-13-78	1B	Mike Flanagan	Baltimore
703	9-13-78	HR-1	Nelson Briles	Baltimore
704	9-13-78	1B	Tim Stoddard	Baltimore
705	9-14-78	HR-1	Scott McGregor	Baltimore
706	9-14-78	1B	Dave Ford	Baltimore
707	9-19-78	2B	Dick Tidrow	at New York
708	9-19-78	HR-1	Dick Tidrow	at New York
709	9-19-78	1B	Dick Tidrow	at New York
710	9-21-78	2B	Dennis Leonard	at Kansas City
711	9-21-78	1B	Dennis Leonard	at Kansas City
712	9-22-78	1B	Matt Keough	Oakland
713	9-23-78	1B	Mike Norris	Oakland
714	9-23-78	2B	Pete Broberg	Oakland
715	9-24-78	2B	Rick Langford	Oakland
716	9-26-78	1B	Don Aase	at California
717	9-29-78	1B	Matt Keough	at Oakland

"I think the future of this team is good. I'm more concerned with doing well for the sake of the team. But everything is falling into place." *— Robin Yount, 1978*

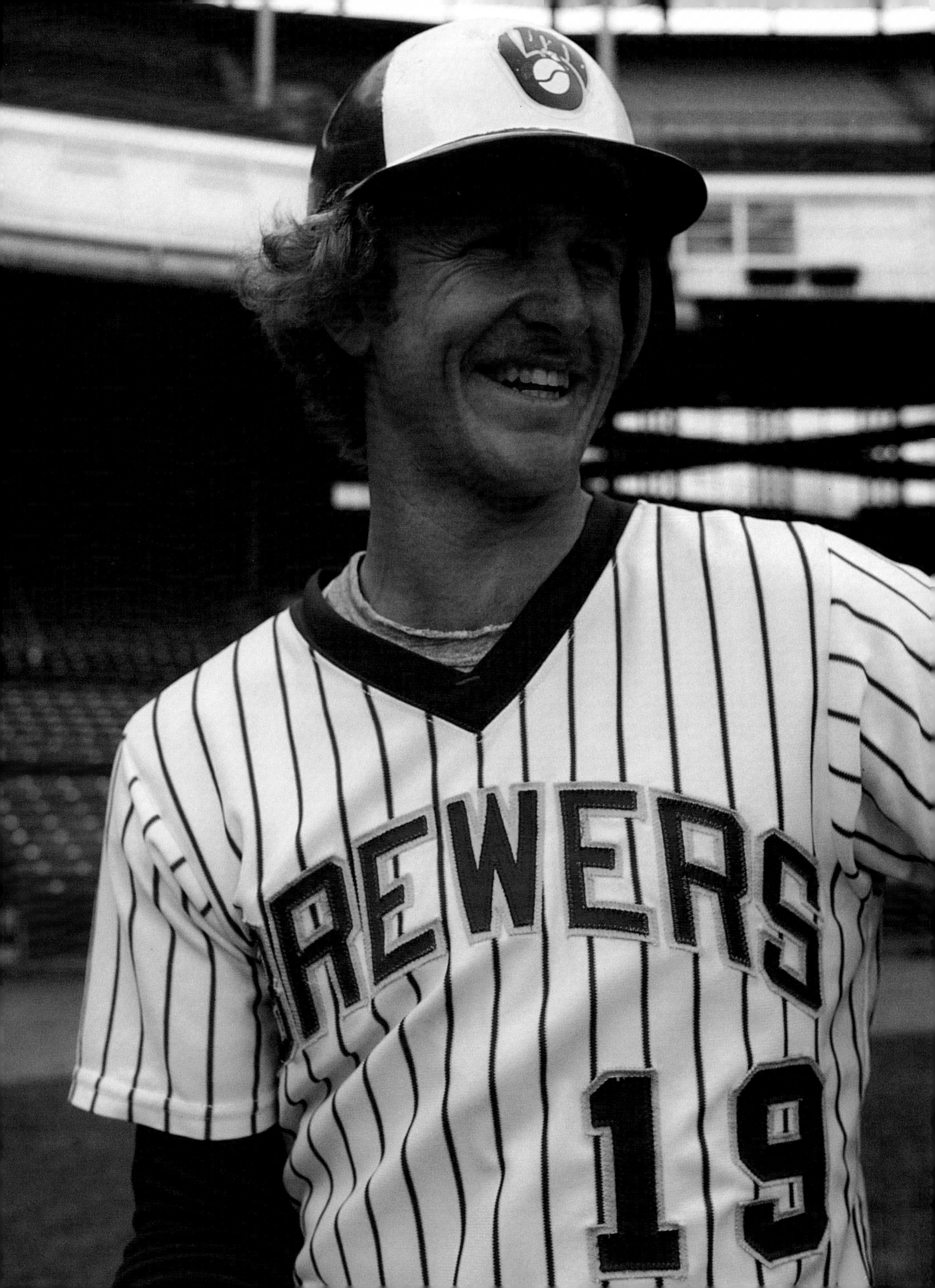
REWERS
19

YOUNT
1979

HIT	DATE	TYPE	PITCHER	OPPONENT
718	4-05-79	1B	Dick Tidrow	at New York
719	4-07-79	1B	Ed Figueroa	at New York
720	4-10-79	1B	Dennis Eckersley	Boston
721	4-10-79	HR-1	Dennis Eckersley	Boston
722	4-13-79	HR-1	Steve Stone	Baltimore
723	4-13-79	1B	Sammy Stewart	Baltimore
724	4-14-79	1B	Dennis Martinez	Baltimore
725	4-14-79	2B	Scott McGregor	Baltimore
726	4-15-79	2B	Jim Palmer	Baltimore
727	4-22-79	2B	Mike Flanagan	at Baltimore
728	4-26-79	2B	Steve Baker	Detroit(2)
729	4-26-79	2B	Bruce Taylor	Detroit
730	4-27-79	2B	Phil Huffman	at Toronto
731	4-30-79	1B	Eric Wilkins	at Cleveland
732	4-30-79	2B	Len Barker	at Cleveland
733	5-01-79	1B	Mike Paxton	at Cleveland
734	5-01-79	1B	Mike Paxton	at Cleveland
735	5-02-79	1B	Wayne Garland	at Cleveland
736	5-02-79	2B	Victor Cruz	at Cleveland
737	5-03-79	1B	Tom Underwood	Toronto
738	5-05-79	1B	Dave Lemanczyk	Toronto
739	5-05-79	1B	Dave Lemanczyk	Toronto
740	5-06-79	HR-1	Mark Lemongello	Toronto
741	5-08-79	1B	Wayne Garland	Cleveland
742	5-08-79	1B	Wayne Garland	Cleveland
743	5-10-79	1B	Eric Wilkins	Cleveland
744	5-11-79	2B	Mark Fidrych	at Detroit
745	5-13-79	1B	Jack Morris	at Detroit
746	5-13-79	1B	Jack Morris	at Detroit
747	5-15-79	1B	Nolan Ryan	at California
748	5-16-79	2B	Dave Frost	at California
749	5-17-79	1B	Don Aase	at California
750	5-19-79	1B	John H. Johnson	at Oakland
751	5-20-79	1B	Dave Heaverlo	at Oakland(1)
752	5-20-79	1B	Steve McCatty	at Oakland(2)
753	5-22-79	2B	Dave Frost	California
754	5-22-79	1B	Dyar Miller	California
755	5-24-79	1B	Chris Knapp	California
756	5-24-79	1B	Mike Barlow	California
757	5-25-79	1B	Bob Lacey	Oakland
758	5-26-79	1B	Rick Langford	Oakland
759	5-26-79	1B	Rick Langford	Oakland
760	5-29-79	2B	Jim Hunter	New York
761	5-30-79	1B	Tommy John	New York
762	5-30-79	1B	Tommy John	New York
763	5-31-79	3B	Luis Tiant	New York
764	5-31-79	1B	Ray Burris	New York
765	6-01-79	HR-1	Larry Gura	at Kansas City
766	6-05-79	2B	Rich Hinton	at Chicago
767	6-12-79	1B	Steve Comer	at Texas
768	6-14-79	1B	Doyle Alexander	at Texas
769	6-14-79	1B	Ed Farmer	at Texas

HIT	DATE	TYPE	PITCHER	OPPONENT
770	6-14-79	1B	Ed Farmer	at Texas
771	6-15-79	1B	Paul Splittorff	Kansas City
772	6-16-79	1B	Steve Busby	Kansas City
773	6-17-79	1B	Rich Gale	Kansas City
774	6-19-79	1B	Dave Goltz	Minnesota
775	6-20-79	1B	Paul Hartzell	Minnesota
776	6-20-79	2B	Darrell Jackson	Minnesota
777	6-21-79	1B	Gary Serum	Minnesota
778	6-22-79	HR-1	Glenn Abbott	at Seattle
779	6-22-79	1B	Rob Dressler	at Seattle
780	6-22-79	2B	Byron McLaughlin	at Seattle
781	6-23-79	1B	Mike Parrott	at Seattle
782	6-23-79	1B	Mike Parrott	at Seattle
783	6-27-79	1B	Gary Serum	at Minnesota
784	6-28-79	1B	Dave Goltz	at Minnesota
785	6-29-79	1B	Glenn Abbott	Seattle
786	6-29-79	2B	Shane Rawley	Seattle
787	6-30-79	1B	Rob Dressler	Seattle
788	6-30-79	1B	Joe Decker	Seattle
789	7-01-79	HR-3	Byron McLaughlin	Seattle
790	7-03-79	1B	Ken Clay	at New York
791	7-05-79	1B	Ron Guidry	at New York
792	7-06-79	1B	Jack Morris	Detroit(1)
793	7-06-79	1B	Jack Morris	Detroit(1)
794	7-08-79	1B	Dan Petry	Detroit(2)
795	7-09-79	1B	Dave Stieb	at Toronto
796	7-09-79	1B	Dave Stieb	at Toronto
797	7-11-79	3B	Tom Buskey	at Toronto
798	7-12-79	1B	Tom Underwood	at Toronto
799	7-13-79	2B	Rick Wise	Cleveland
800	7-14-79	1B	David Clyde	Cleveland
801	7-14-79	1B	Paul Reuschel	Cleveland
802	7-15-79	3B	Len Barker	Cleveland
803	7-15-79	1B	Dan Spillner	Cleveland
804	7-20-79	1B	Tom Underwood	Toronto
805	7-21-79	1B	Len Barker	at Cleveland
806	7-22-79	HR-2	Mike Paxton	at Cleveland(1)
807	7-22-79	1B	Paul Reuschel	at Cleveland(1)
808	7-22-79	1B	Paul Reuschel	at Cleveland(1)
809	7-23-79	1B	Dan Spillner	at Cleveland
810	7-23-79	2B	Dan Spillner	at Cleveland
811	7-26-79	1B	Dan Petry	at Detroit
812	7-28-79	1B	Luis Tiant	New York
813	7-28-79	1B	Ray Burris	New York
814	7-29-79	3B	Jim Hunter	New York
815	7-29-79	1B	Jim Kaat	New York
816	7-31-79	1B	Mike Flanagan	Baltimore
817	7-31-79	1B	Mike Flanagan	Baltimore
818	8-01-79	1B	Dennis Martinez	Baltimore
819	8-01-79	1B	Dennis Martinez	Baltimore
820	8-04-79	1B	Allen Ripley	Boston

HIT	DATE	TYPE	PITCHER	OPPONENT
821	8-05-79	3B	Dennis Eckersley	Boston(1)
822	8-07-79	2B	Scott McGregor	at Baltimore
823	8-08-79	1B	Steve Stone	at Baltimore
824	8-09-79	1B	Mike Flanagan	at Baltimore
825	8-10-79	1B	Dick Drago	at Boston
826	8-11-79	1B	Mike Torrez	at Boston
827	8-13-79	2B	Larry Gura	Kansas City
828	8-14-79	1B	Dennis Leonard	Kansas City
829	8-15-79	1B	Rich Gale	Kansas City
830	8-16-79	1B	Brian Allard	Texas
831	8-17-79	2B	Steve Comer	Texas
832	8-18-79	1B	Ferguson Jenkins	Texas
833	8-19-79	1B	Doc Medich	Texas
834	8-21-79	2B	Fred Howard	Chicago(2)
835	8-21-79	1B	Guy Hoffman	Chicago(2)
836	8-27-79	HR-3	Dan Quisenberry	at Kansas City
837	8-28-79	1B	Craig Chamberlain	at Kansas City
838	8-28-79	1B	Steve Busby	at Kansas City
839	8-28-79	1B	Dan Quisenberry	at Kansas City
840	8-29-79	1B	Marty Pattin	at Kansas City
841	8-30-79	2B	Randy Scarbery	at Chicago
842	8-30-79	1B	Ed Farmer	at Chicago
843	8-31-79	1B	Steve Trout	at Chicago
844	9-03-79	1B	Mike Norris	at Oakland
845	9-03-79	1B	Jackson Todd	at Oakland
846	9-05-79	1B	Matt Keough	at Oakland
847	9-05-79	1B	Matt Keough	at Oakland
848	9-08-79	1B	Jim Barr	at California
849	9-09-79	1B	Dave LaRoche	at California
850	9-12-79	1B	Mike Morgan	Oakland
851	9-12-79	1B	Mike Morgan	Oakland
852	9-12-79	1B	Dave Heaverlo	Oakland
853	9-13-79	1B	Steve McCatty	Oakland
854	9-13-79	1B	Steve McCatty	Oakland
855	9-14-79	2B	Jim Barr	California
856	9-14-79	1B	Jim Barr	California
857	9-14-79	2B	John Montague	California
858	9-15-79	1B	Frank Tanana	California
859	9-17-79	1B	Rick Honeycutt	at Seattle
860	9-19-79	1B	Floyd Bannister	at Seattle
861	9-19-79	1B	Glenn Abbott	at Seattle
862	9-21-79	1B	Jerry Koosman	Minnesota
863	9-21-79	1B	Mike Marshall	Minnesota
864	9-22-79	1B	Roger Erickson	Minnesota
865	9-22-79	2B	Roger Erickson	Minnesota
866	9-23-79	1B	Pete Redfern	Minnesota
867	9-25-79	1B	Floyd Bannister	Seattle
868	9-25-79	1B	Floyd Bannister	Seattle
869	9-26-79	1B	Mike Parrott	Seattle
870	9-27-79	1B	Byron McLaughlin	Seattle
871	9-30-79	1B	Jerry Koosman	at Minnesota

"I never approach this game looking down the road to accomplish anything other than the wins." *— Robin Yount, 1979*

1000
1980

HIT	DATE	TYPE	PITCHER	OPPONENT
872	4-12-80	1B	Mike Torrez	Boston
873	4-12-80	HR-1	Chuck Rainey	Boston
874	4-13-80	2B	Bob Stanley	Boston
875	4-13-80	1B	Bob Stanley	Boston
876	4-18-80	1B	Luis Tiant	at New York
877	4-18-80	2B	Luis Tiant	at New York
878	4-18-80	3B	Ron Davis	at New York
879	4-19-80	1B	Ed Figueroa	at New York
880	4-19-80	2B	Rich Gossage	at New York
881	4-20-80	1B	Ron Guidry	at New York
882	4-20-80	1B	Ron Guidry	at New York
883	4-21-80	2B	Bob Owchinko	Cleveland
884	4-21-80	2B	Bob Owchinko	Cleveland
885	4-22-80	3B	Len Barker	Cleveland
886	4-22-80	1B	Mike Paxton	Cleveland
887	4-23-80	1B	Dan Spillner	Cleveland
888	4-23-80	2B	Dan Spillner	Cleveland
889	4-25-80	1B	Dave Lemanczyk	Toronto
890	4-25-80	1B	Joey McLaughlin	Toronto
891	4-26-80	1B	Dave Stieb	Toronto
892	4-27-80	1B	Paul Mirabella	Toronto
893	4-27-80	2B	Paul Mirabella	Toronto
894	5-03-80	1B	Britt Burns	at Chicago
895	5-04-80	HR-4	Rich Wortham	at Chicago
896	5-05-80	1B	Rich Dotson	at Chicago
897	5-05-80	1B	Rich Dotson	at Chicago
898	5-05-80	HR-1	Mike Proly	at Chicago
899	5-07-80	1B	Tommy John	New York
900	5-08-80	1B	Dennis Martinez	Balitmore
901	5-08-80	1B	Paul Hartzell	Baltimore
902	5-09-80	2B	Steve Stone	Baltimore
903	5-09-80	1B	Dave Ford	Baltimore
904	5-10-80	1B	Scott McGregor	Baltimore
905	5-11-80	2B	Mike Flanagan	Baltimore
906	5-13-80	HR-1	Britt Burns	Chicago
907	5-14-80	2B	Mike Proly	Chicago
908	5-14-80	3B	Mike Proly	Chicago
909	5-14-80	1B	Mike Proly	Chicago
910	5-15-80	1B	Rich Dotson	Chicago
911	5-15-80	1B	Ed Farmer	Chicago
912	5-17-80	2B	Geoff Zahn	at Minnesota
913	5-17-80	2B	John Verhoeven	at Minnesota
914	5-17-80	1B	John Verhoeven	at Minnesota
915	5-19-80	HR-2	Glenn Abbott	at Seattle
916	5-20-80	HR-1	Floyd Bannister	at Seattle
917	5-20-80	1B	Dave Roberts	at Seattle
918	5-20-80	1B	Dave Heaverlo	at Seattle
919	5-23-80	HR-2	Pete Redfern	Minnesota
920	5-24-80	1B	Jerry Koosman	Minnesota
921	5-26-80	1B	Mike Parrott	Seattle
922	5-26-80	2B	Rob Dressler	Seattle
923	5-27-80	1B	Jim Beattie	Seattle
924	5-27-80	1B	Jim Beattie	Seattle
925	5-28-80	2B	Bryon McLaughlin	Seattle
926	5-30-80	1B	Chuck Rainey	at Boston
927	5-31-80	1B	Keith MacWhorter	at Boston
928	5-31-80	HR-1	Dick Drago	at Boston
929	5-31-80	2B	Skip Lockwood	at Boston
930	6-01-80	1B	Tom Burgmeier	at Boston
931	6-01-80	1B	Tom Burgmeier	at Boston
932	6-01-80	2B	Dick Drago	at Boston
933	6-02-80	2B	Steve Stone	at Baltimore
934	6-06-80	2B	Pat Underwood	Detroit
935	6-06-80	1B	Pat Underwood	Detroit
936	6-07-80	3B	Jack Morris	Detroit
937	6-07-80	1B	Jack Morris	Detroit
938	6-08-80	2B	Aurelio Lopez	Detroit
939	6-10-80	HR-1	Ferguson Jenkins	Texas
940	6-11-80	2B	Jon Matlack	Texas
941	6-12-80	1B	Gaylord Perry	Texas
942	6-13-80	1B	Larry Gura	Kansas City
943	6-13-80	1B	Larry Gura	Kansas City
944	6-14-80	HR-2	Renie Martin	Kansas City
945	6-14-80	1B	Rawly Eastwick	Kansas City
946	6-15-80	HR-1	Dennis Leonard	Kansas City
947	6-16-80	2B	Milt Wilcox	at Detroit(1)
948	6-16-80	1B	Milt Wilcox	at Detroit(1)
949	6-16-80	1B	Dave Rozema	at Detroit(2)
950	6-28-80	1B	Ed Halicki	at California
951	6-28-80	1B	Fred Martinez	at California
952	6-28-80	1B	Ed Hassler	at California
953	6-29-80	2B	Don Aase	at California
954	6-29-80	1B	Don Aase	at California
955	7-01-80	HR-1	Steve McCatty	Oakland
956	7-01-80	HR-1	Steve McCatty	Oakland
957	7-01-80	2B	Steve McCatty	Oakland
958	7-02-80	1B	Mike Norris	Oakland
959	7-03-80	1B	Matt Keough	Oakland
960	7-03-80	1B	Matt Keough	Oakland
961	7-05-80	2B	Chris Knapp	California
962	7-06-80	2B	Ed Halicki	California
963	7-10-80	1B	Steve Renko	Boston(2)
964	7-12-80	2B	Jesse Jefferson	at Toronto
965	7-12-80	3B	Mike Barlow	at Toronto
966	7-14-80	HR-3	Jerry Garvin	at Toronto
967	7-16-80	2B	Jim Palmer	Baltimore
968	7-18-80	3B	Steve Trout	Chicago
969	7-18-80	1B	Steve Trout	Chicago
970	7-18-80	HR-1	Steve Trout	Chicago
971	7-19-80	1B	Lamarr Hoyt	Chicago
972	7-19-80	1B	Lamarr Hoyt	Chicago
973	7-20-80	3B	Rich Dotson	Chicago
974	7-20-80	2B	Mike Proly	Chicago
975	7-21-80	1B	Tom Underwood	at New York
976	7-21-80	1B	Tom Underwood	at New York
977	7-21-80	1B	Ron Davis	at New York
978	7-22-80	1B	Rudy May	at New York(2)
979	7-23-80	2B	Ron Guidry	at New York
980	7-25-80	1B	Jim Palmer	at Baltimore
981	7-26-80	1B	Steve Stone	at Baltimore
982	7-26-80	2B	Steve Stone	at Baltimore
983	7-29-80	1B	Rich Dotson	at Chicago
984	7-29-80	1B	Guy Hoffman	at Chicago
985	7-31-80	2B	Tommy John	New York
986	7-31-80	2B	Tommy John	New York
987	8-02-80	HR-1	Rudy May	New York
988	8-02-80	1B	Rich Gossage	New York
989	8-02-80	1B	Rich Gossage	New York
990	8-06-80	HR-1	Win Remmerswaal	at Boston
991	8-06-80	2B	Bill Campbell	at Boston
992	8-07-80	2B	Mike Torrez	at Boston
993	8-12-80	1B	Jim Clancy	Toronto(1)
994	8-12-80	HR-2	Jack Kucek	Toronto(2)
995	8-12-80	1B	Mike Barlow	Toronto(2)
996	8-13-80	2B	Jackson Todd	Toronto
997	8-13-80	1B	Jackson Todd	Toronto
998	8-13-80	1B	Joey McLaughlin	Toronto
999	8-16-80	HR-4	Dan Spillner	at Cleveland
1000	8-16-80	2B	Sandy Wihtol	at Cleveland
1001	8-16-80	2B	Mike Stanton	at Cleveland
1002	8-17-80	2B	Bob Owchinko	at Cleveland(2)
1003	8-18-80	1B	Dan Petry	Detroit
1004	8-18-80	1B	Dan Petry	Detroit
1005	8-18-80	2B	Dan Petry	Detroit
1006	8-20-80	1B	Jerry Udjur	Detroit
1007	8-22-80	3B	Doc Medich	at Texas(2)
1008	8-22-80	1B	Charlie Hough	at Texas(2)
1009	8-23-80	2B	Ed Figueroa	at Texas
1010	8-24-80	1B	Jon Matlack	at Texas
1011	8-26-80	1B	Dan Quisenberry	Kansas City
1012	8-27-80	1B	Paul Splittorff	Kansas City
1013	8-27-80	2B	Paul Splittorff	Kansas City
1014	8-27-80	HR-1	Paul Splittorff	Kansas City
1015	8-28-80	2B	Bruce Robbins	at Detroit
1016	8-28-80	3B	Jerry Udjur	at Detroit
1017	8-29-80	1B	Milt Wilcox	at Detroit
1018	8-31-80	3B	Jerry Udjur	at Detroit
1019	9-01-80	2B	Rich Gale	at Kansas City
1020	9-01-80	1B	Rich Gale	at Kansas City
1021	9-03-80	2B	Dennis Leonard	at Kansas City
1022	9-04-80	1B	Larry Gura	at Kansas City
1023	9-04-80	2B	Larry Gura	at Kansas City
1024	9-04-80	1B	Dan Quisenberry	at Kansas City
1025	9-06-80	2B	Ken Clay	Texas
1026	9-06-80	1B	Don Kainer	Texas
1027	9-12-80	1B	Floyd Bannister	at Seattle
1028	9-12-80	2B	Floyd Bannister	at Seattle
1029	9-12-80	HR-2	Byron McLaughlin	at Seattle
1030	9-13-80	1B	Mike Parrott	at Seattle
1031	9-14-80	1B	Rick Honeycutt	at Seattle
1032	9-17-80	1B	Jerry Koosman	Minnesota
1033	9-18-80	1B	Geoff Zahn	Minnesota(1)
1034	9-18-80	1B	Pete Redfern	Minnesota(2)
1035	9-18-80	1B	Bob Veselic	Minnesota(2)
1036	9-19-80	1B	Rick Honeycutt	Seattle
1037	9-20-80	1B	Rob Dressler	Seattle
1038	9-20-80	1B	Mike Parrott	Seattle
1039	9-21-80	HR-1	Glenn Abbott	Seattle
1040	9-23-80	1B	Fred Martinez	California
1041	9-24-80	1B	Frank Tanana	California
1042	9-26-80	HR-1	Mike Norris	at Oakland
1043	9-26-80	1B	Mike Norris	at Oakland
1044	9-27-80	1B	Rick Langford	at Oakland
1045	9-28-80	1B	Steve McCatty	at Oakland
1046	9-29-80	1B	Frank Tanana	at California
1047	9-30-80	2B	Dave LaRoche	at California
1048	10-1-80	2B	Ed Halicki	at California
1049	10-2-80	1B	Chris Knapp	at California
1050	10-5-80	1B	Dave Beard	Oakland

"The only way I get the most out of myself is to push myself as hard as I can, every pitch of every inning of every game." *— Robin Yount, 1980*

ROBIN
1981

HIT	DATE	TYPE	PITCHER	OPPONENT
1051	4-12-81	1B	John Denny	at Cleveland
1052	4-12-81	2B	John Denny	at Cleveland
1053	4-13-81	1B	Ross Baumgarten	at Chicago
1054	4-20-81	2B	Jackson Todd	at Toronto
1055	4-21-81	1B	Dave Stieb	at Toronto
1056	4-22-81	1B	Luis Leal	at Toronto
1057	4-22-81	3B	Jerry Garvin	at Toronto
1058	4-25-81	1B	Larry Gura	Kansas City
1059	4-27-81	2B	Luis Leal	Toronto
1060	4-27-81	1B	Luis Leal	Toronto
1061	4-28-81	1B	Mark Bomback	Toronto
1062	4-28-81	1B	Joey McLaughlin	Toronto
1063	4-30-81	3B	John D'Acquisto	at California
1064	4-30-81	1B	John D'Acquisto	at California
1065	5-02-81	1B	Andy Hassler	at California
1066	5-03-81	2B	Steve Renko	at California
1067	5-03-81	1B	Steve Renko	at California
1068	5-04-81	HR-2	Brian Allard	at Seattle
1069	5-04-81	HR-1	Brian Allard	at Seattle
1070	5-04-81	1B	Dick Drago	at Seattle
1071	5-05-81	HR-3	Jerry Don Gleaton	at Seattle
1072	5-05-81	1B	Jerry Don Gleaton	at Seattle
1073	5-05-81	2B	Jerry Don Gleaton	at Seattle
1074	5-20-81	1B	Al Williams	Minnesota
1075	5-23-81	1B	Mike Torrez	Boston
1076	5-24-81	1B	Frank Tanana	Boston(1)
1077	5-24-81	1B	Bob Stanley	Boston(2)
1078	5-26-81	1B	Aurelio Lopez	Detroit
1079	5-27-81	1B	Howard Bailey	Detroit
1080	5-27-81	1B	Dave Tobik	Detroit
1081	5-28-81	1B	Dan Petry	Detroit
1082	5-29-81	HR-1	Mike Torrez	at Boston
1083	5-29-81	1B	Mike Torrez	at Boston
1084	5-31-81	1B	Tom Burgmeier	at Boston
1085	6-02-81	1B	Dan Petry	at Detroit
1086	6-02-81	1B	George Cappuzello	at Detroit
1087	6-03-81	1B	Dan Schatzeder	at Detroit
1088	6-03-81	1B	Dan Schatzeder	at Detroit
1089	6-03-81	1B	Dan Schatzeder	at Detroit
1090	6-05-81	HR-1	Larry Gura	at Kansas City
1091	6-05-81	3B	Larry Gura	at Kansas City
1092	6-06-81	1B	Paul Splittorff	at Kansas City
1093	6-10-81	1B	Doc Medich	Texas
1094	6-11-81	1B	Ferguson Jenkins	Texas
1095	6-11-81	1B	Ferguson Jenkins	Texas
1096	8-10-81	2B	Bert Blyleven	at Cleveland
1097	8-11-81	HR-1	John Denny	at Cleveland(1)
1098	8-11-81	1B	Dan Spillner	at Cleveland(2)
1099	8-11-81	1B	Dan Spillner	at Cleveland(2)
1100	8-12-81	2B	Len Barker	at Cleveland
1101	8-13-81	1B	Sid Monge	at Cleveland
1102	8-14-81	1B	Jim Clancy	at Toronto
1103	8-14-81	1B	Luis Leal	at Toronto
1104	8-14-81	1B	Jerry Garvin	at Toronto
1105	8-15-81	1B	Mark Bomback	at Toronto
1106	8-16-81	2B	Dave Stieb	at Toronto
1107	8-16-81	1B	Paul Mirabella	at Toronto
1108	8-18-81	1B	Jon Matlack	at Texas(1)
1109	8-19-81	1B	Doc Medich	at Texas
1110	8-22-81	1B	Jack O'Connor	Minnesota
1111	8-23-81	HR-1	John Verhoeven	Minnesota
1112	8-25-81	2B	Dennis Lamp	Chicago
1113	8-28-81	1B	Charlie Hough	Texas
1114	8-30-81	1B	Doc Medich	Texas
1115	9-01-81	1B	Larry Gura	at Kansas City
1116	9-02-81	1B	Dan Quisenberry	at Kansas City
1117	9-03-81	1B	Brad Havens	at Minnesota
1118	9-03-81	1B	Brad Havens	at Minnesota
1119	9-04-81	HR-2	Jack O'Connor	at Minnesota
1120	9-05-81	1B	Al Williams	at Minnesota
1121	9-06-81	1B	Pete Redfern	at Minnesota
1122	9-07-81	HR-1	Ron Guidry	at New York
1123	9-09-81	1B	Tommy John	at New York
1124	9-10-81	1B	Ross Baumgarten	Chicago
1125	9-11-81	1B	Dennis Martinez	Balitmore
1126	9-11-81	1B	Dennis Martinez	Baltimore
1127	9-14-81	1B	Tommy John	New York
1128	9-14-81	1B	Tommy John	New York
1129	9-15-81	1B	Rudy May	New York
1130	9-19-81	1B	Dennis Martinez	at Baltimore
1131	9-19-81	1B	Dennis Martinez	at Baltimore
1132	9-19-81	1B	Tippy Martinez	at Baltimore
1133	9-21-81	2B	Dennis Eckersley	at Boston
1134	9-21-81	1B	Dennis Eckersley	at Boston
1135	9-22-81	2B	Mark Clear	at Boston
1136	9-23-81	1B	Frank Tanana	at Boston
1137	9-23-81	1B	Frank Tanana	at Boston
1138	9-25-81	HR-3	Jack Morris	at Detroit
1139	9-26-81	1B	Milt Wilcox	at Detroit
1140	9-27-81	2B	Dan Petry	at Detroit
1141	9-27-81	1B	Dan Petry	at Detroit
1142	9-28-81	1B	Frank Tanana	Boston
1143	9-29-81	1B	Mike Torrez	Boston
1144	9-29-81	3B	Mike Torrez	Boston
1145	9-30-81	2B	Bruce Hurst	Boston
1146	9-30-81	3B	Bruce Hurst	Boston
1147	9-30-81	1B	Bob Stanley	Boston
1148	9-30-81	1B	Bill Campbell	Boston
1149	10-2-81	2B	Dan Petry	Detroit
1150	10-2-81	1B	Dan Petry	Detroit
1151	10-2-81	1B	Dave Rozema	Detroit
1152	10-3-81	1B	Jack Morris	Detroit
1153	10-5-81	1B	Milt Wilcox	Detroit

"What I want to do more than anything is play in a World Series."

— Robin Yount, 1981

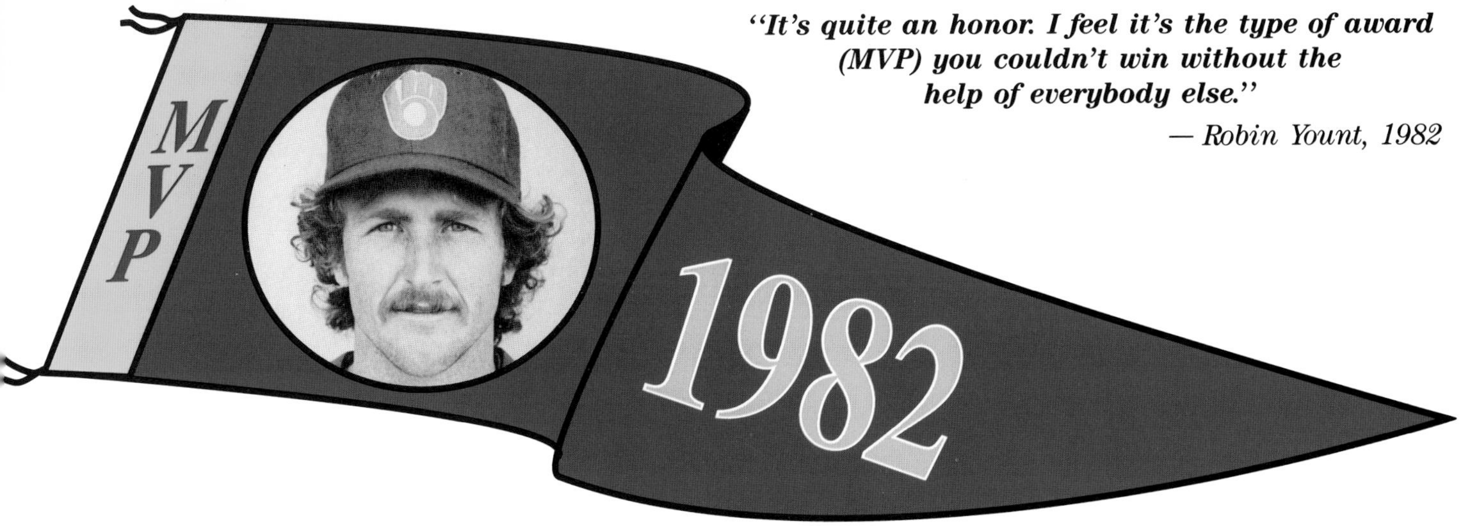
MVP
1982

"It's quite an honor. I feel it's the type of award (MVP) you couldn't win without the help of everybody else."

— Robin Yount, 1982

HIT	DATE	TYPE	PITCHER	OPPONENT
1154	4-09-82	1B	Mark Bomback	at Toronto
1155	4-09-82	1B	Dale Murray	at Toronto
1156	4-09-82	2B	Jerry Garvin	at Toronto
1157	4-11-82	2B	Jerry Garvin	at Toronto
1158	4-13-82	HR-1	Lary Sorensen	at Cleveland
1159	4-13-82	2B	Lary Sorensen	at Cleveland
1160	4-13-82	1B	Rick Sutcliffe	at Cleveland
1161	4-18-82	2B	Jon Matlack	Texas
1162	4-24-82	1B	Dave Schmidt	at Texas
1163	4-25-82	1B	Charlie Hough	at Texas
1164	4-25-82	1B	Jon Matlack	at Texas
1165	4-25-82	1B	Danny Darwin	at Texas
1166	4-25-82	1B	Danny Darwin	at Texas
1167	4-27-82	1B	Lamarr Hoyt	Chicago
1168	4-30-82	2B	Ron Davis	at Minnesota
1169	5-01-82	1B	Brad Havens	at Minnesota
1170	5-01-82	1B	Brad Havens	at Minnesota
1171	5-02-82	1B	Brad Corbett	at Minnesota
1172	5-04-82	1B	Larry Gura	Kansas City
1173	5-05-82	2B	Vida Blue	Kansas City
1174	5-05-82	1B	Dan Quisenberry	Kansas City
1175	5-06-82	3B	Brad Havens	Minnesota
1176	5-08-82	3B	Terry Felton	Minnesota
1177	5-08-82	1B	Terry Felton	Minnesota
1178	5-08-82	1B	Darrell Jackson	Minnesota
1179	5-10-82	2B	Vida Blue	at Kansas City
1180	5-10-82	2B	Vida Blue	at Kansas City
1181	5-11-82	1B	Larry Gura	at Kansas City
1182	5-13-82	1B	Lamarr Hoyt	at Chicago
1183	5-13-82	1B	Lamarr Hoyt	at Chicago
1184	5-13-82	HR-1	Lamarr Hoyt	at Chicago
1185	5-15-82	3B	Jerry Koosman	at Chicago
1186	5-16-82	1B	Steve Trout	at Chicago
1187	5-19-82	1B	Bruce Kison	California
1188	5-21-82	1B	Gaylord Perry	Seattle
1189	5-21-82	1B	Gaylord Perry	Seattle
1190	5-22-82	1B	Gene Nelson	Seattle
1191	5-25-82	2B	Matt Keough	Oakland
1192	5-25-82	2B	Dave Beard	Oakland
1193	5-26-82	2B	Tom Underwood	Oakland
1194	5-27-82	1B	Ken Forsch	at California
1195	5-28-82	1B	Geoff Zahn	at California
1196	5-28-82	1B	Geoff Zahn	at California
1197	5-28-82	2B	Geoff Zahn	at California
1198	5-29-82	3B	Steve Renko	at California
1199	5-29-82	1B	Andy Hassler	at California
1200	5-31-82	HR-1	Gaylord Perry	at Seattle
1201	5-31-82	HR-1	Gaylord Perry	at Seattle
1202	6-01-82	2B	Gene Nelson	at Seattle
1203	6-02-82	1B	Floyd Bannister	at Seattle
1204	6-04-82	2B	Matt Keough	at Oakland
1205	6-05-82	2B	Dave Beard	at Oakland
1206	6-05-82	1B	Dave Beard	at Oakland
1207	6-05-82	HR-1	Dave Beard	at Oakland
1208	6-06-82	1B	Tom Underwood	at Oakland
1209	6-07-82	HR-1	Jim Palmer	Baltimore
1210	6-08-82	2B	Scott McGregor	Baltimore
1211	6-10-82	1B	Storm Davis	Baltimore
1212	6-11-82	1B	Dan Petry	Detroit
1213	6-11-82	1B	Aurelio Lopez	Detroit
1214	6-13-82	1B	Pat Underwood	Detroit
1215	6-13-82	1B	Pat Underwood	Detroit
1216	6-13-82	HR-3	Elias Sosa	Detroit
1217	6-14-82	1B	Scott McGregor	at Baltimore
1218	6-15-82	HR-2	Mike Flanagan	at Baltimore
1219	6-15-82	3B	Mike Flanagan	at Baltimore
1220	6-16-82	HR-1	Dennis Martinez	at Baltimore
1221	6-16-82	1B	Dennis Martinez	at Baltimore
1222	6-18-82	2B	Milt Wilcox	at Detroit
1223	6-18-82	1B	Milt Wilcox	at Detroit
1224	6-19-82	HR-2	Jack Morris	at Detroit
1225	6-19-82	HR-2	Aurelio Lopez	at Detroit
1226	6-21-82	1B	Dave Righetti	New York
1227	6-22-82	3B	Roger Erickson	New York
1228	6-25-82	1B	Luis Aponte	at Boston
1229	6-26-82	2B	Bob Stanley	at Boston
1230	6-26-82	1B	Bob Stanley	at Boston
1231	6-27-82	1B	Mike Torrez	at Boston
1232	6-27-82	3B	Mike Torrez	at Boston
1233	6-27-82	1B	Tom Burgmeier	at Boston
1234	6-28-82	1B	Chuck Rainey	at Boston
1235	6-29-82	1B	Ron Guidry	at New York
1236	6-20-82	3B	Tommy John	at New York
1237	6-20-82	1B	Tommy John	at New York
1238	7-01-82	1B	Mike Morgan	at New York
1239	7-02-82	1B	Mike Torrez	Boston
1240	7-02-82	1B	Mike Torrez	Boston
1241	7-02-82	2B	Mike Torrez	Boston
1242	7-02-82	1B	Mike Torrez	Boston
1243	7-02-82	1B	Tom Burgmeier	Boston
1244	7-03-82	HR-3	Chuck Rainey	Boston
1245	7-04-82	1B	Dennis Eckersley	Boston
1246	7-04-82	1B	Dennis Eckersley	Boston
1247	7-05-82	1B	Lamarr Hoyt	at Chicago
1248	7-05-82	HR-2	Lamarr Hoyt	at Chicago
1249	7-07-82	HR-2	Brad Havens	Minnesota
1250	7-07-82	1B	Brad Havens	Minnesota
1251	7-07-82	1B	Jeff Little	Minnesota
1252	7-09-82	2B	Paul Splittorff	Kansas City
1253	7-09-82	1B	Paul Splittorff	Kansas City
1254	7-10-82	1B	Vida Blue	Kansas City
1255	7-10-82	HR-1	Vida Blue	Kansas City
1256	7-11-82	2B	Larry Gura	Kansas City
1257	7-11-82	1B	Dan Quisenberry	Kansas City
1258	7-15-82	2B	Rich Dotson	Chicago(1)
1259	7-15-82	2B	Lamarr Hoyt	Chicago(2)
1260	7-18-82	2B	Richard Barnes	Chicago
1261	7-18-82	2B	Ernesto Escarrega	Chicago
1262	7-19-82	1B	Al Williams	at Minnesota
1263	7-19-82	HR-1	Al Williams	at Minnesota
1264	7-19-82	1B	John Pacella	at Minnesota
1265	7-19-82	HR-2	John Pacella	at Minnesota
1266	7-20-82	1B	Jack O'Connor	at Minnesota
1267	7-21-82	1B	Frank Viola	at Minnesota
1268	7-21-82	1B	Jeff Little	at Minnesota
1269	7-23-82	2B	Paul Splittorff	at Kansas City
1270	7-23-82	1B	Paul Splittorff	at Kansas City
1271	7-23-82	1B	Paul Splittorff	at Kansas City
1272	7-24-82	3B	Derek Botelho	at Kansas City
1273	7-24-82	1B	Derek Botelho	at Kansas City
1274	7-25-82	HR-1	Larry Gura	at Kansas City
1275	7-25-82	HR-1	Larry Gura	at Kansas City
1276	7-26-82	1B	Charlie Hough	at Texas
1277	7-27-82	1B	Dan Boitano	at Texas
1278	7-28-82	2B	Frank Tanana	at Texas
1279	7-28-82	1B	Frank Tanana	at Texas
1280	7-29-82	2B	Len Barker	Cleveland
1281	7-29-82	2B	Len Barker	Cleveland
1282	7-30-82	1B	Lary Sorensen	Cleveland
1283	7-31-82	1B	Rick Waits	Cleveland
1284	8-01-82	2B	Bud Anderson	Cleveland(2)
1285	8-03-82	1B	Jim Clancy	at Toronto
1286	8-04-82	1B	Jerry Garvin	at Toronto
1287	8-08-82	1B	Len Barker	at Cleveland
1288	8-09-82	2B	Doc Medich	Texas
1289	8-10-82	2B	Charlie Hough	Texas
1290	8-10-82	1B	Charlie Hough	Texas
1291	8-11-82	1B	Rick Honeycutt	Texas
1292	8-12-82	1B	Ken Schrom	Toronto(1)
1293	8-13-82	1B	Luis Leal	Toronto
1294	8-13-82	1B	Luis Leal	Toronto
1295	8-14-82	2B	Dave Stieb	Toronto
1296	8-15-82	HR-1	Jim Clancy	Toronto
1297	8-17-82	1B	Rick Langford	at Oakland
1298	8-17-82	HR-1	Rick Langford	at Oakland
1299	8-17-82	HR-2	Rick Langford	at Oakland
1300	8-19-82	2B	Matt Keough	at Oakland
1301	8-19-82	2B	Bob Owchinko	at Oakland
1302	8-20-82	1B	Mike Moore	at Seattle
1303	8-20-82	1B	Mike Moore	at Seattle
1304	8-22-82	1B	Floyd Bannister	at Seattle
1305	8-22-82	1B	Bill Caudill	at Seattle
1306	8-23-82	1B	Mike Witt	at California
1307	8-23-82	1B	Mike Witt	at California
1308	8-24-82	2B	Steve Renko	at California
1309	8-24-82	1B	Steve Renko	at California
1310	8-24-82	2B	Dave Goltz	at California
1311	8-24-82	HR-2	Andy Hassler	at California
1312	8-26-82	3B	Bob Owchinko	Oakland
1313	8-26-82	2B	Bob Owchinko	Oakland
1314	8-26-82	2B	Preston Hanna	Oakland
1315	8-27-82	1B	Preston Hanna	Oakland
1316	8-28-82	1B	Rick Langford	Oakland
1317	8-29-82	1B	Mike Norris	Oakland
1318	8-29-82	1B	Mike Norris	Oakland
1319	8-29-82	1B	Mike Norris	Oakland
1320	8-31-82	2B	Bryan Clark	Seattle
1321	9-01-82	1B	Mike Stanton	Seattle
1322	9-02-82	2B	Ed Whitson	Cleveland(2)
1323	9-02-82	1B	Dan Spillner	Cleveland(2)
1324	9-04-82	1B	Luis Tiant	California
1325	9-04-82	1B	Luis Tiant	California
1326	9-05-82	1B	Ricky Steirer	California
1327	9-06-82	1B	Milt Wilcox	Detroit
1328	9-07-82	1B	Dan Petry	Detroit
1329	9-07-82	2B	Dan Petry	Detroit
1330	9-07-82	1B	Dan Petry	Detroit
1331	9-08-82	1B	Jerry Udjur	Detroit
1332	9-09-82	1B	Shane Rawley	at New York
1333	9-10-82	1B	Ron Guidry	at New York
1334	9-13-82	2B	Jerry Udjur	at Detroit
1335	9-13-82	1B	Jerry Udjur	at Detroit
1336	9-14-82	1B	Dave Rucker	at Detroit
1337	9-14-82	1B	Dave Rucker	at Detroit
1338	9-15-82	2B	Jack Morris	at Detroit
1339	9-17-82	2B	Stefan Wever	New York
1340	9-17-82	1B	Stefan Wever	New York
1341	9-17-82	1B	George Frazier	New York
1342	9-17-82	HR-1	Doyle Alexander	New York
1343	9-18-82	1B	Jay Howell	New York
1344	9-18-82	1B	Jay Howell	New York
1345	9-18-82	1B	Mike Morgan	New York
1346	9-19-82	1B	Shane Rawley	New York
1347	9-19-82	3B	Shane Rawley	New York
1348	9-20-82	1B	Bob Stanley	Boston
1349	9-24-82	HR-2	Mike Flanagan	Baltimore
1350	9-24-82	1B	Mike Flanagan	Baltimore
1351	9-24-82	HR-3	Don Stanhouse	Baltimore
1352	9-26-82	1B	Dennis Martinez	Baltimore
1353	9-28-82	HR-2	Chuck Rainey	at Boston
1354	9-28-82	1B	Chuck Rainey	at Boston
1355	9-28-82	1B	Bruce Hurst	at Boston
1356	9-30-82	2B	Dennis Eckersley	at Boston
1357	9-30-82	1B	Dennis Eckersley	at Boston
1358	10-1-82	1B	Dennis Martinez	at Baltimore
1359	10-1-82	1B	Dennis Martinez	at Baltimore
1360	10-1-82	1B	Dennis Martinez	at Baltimore
1361	10-3-82	HR-1	Jim Palmer	at Baltimore
1362	10-3-82	HR-1	Jim Palmer	at Baltimore
1363	10-3-82	3B	Tippy Martinez	at Baltimore

BREWERS

ROBIN
1983

HIT	DATE	TYPE	PITCHER	OPPONENT
1364	4-05-83	1B	Luis Sanchez	at California
1365	4-06-83	1B	Tommy John	at California
1366	4-07-83	HR-2	Mike Witt	at California
1367	4-08-83	3B	Larry Gura	at Kansas City
1368	4-10-83	2B	Mike Armstrong	at Kansas City
1369	4-10-83	HR-1	Bill Castro	at Kansas City
1370	4-12-83	HR-2	Luis Leal	at Toronto
1371	4-12-83	1B	Mike Morgan	at Toronto
1372	4-13-83	1B	Jim Clancy	at Toronto
1373	4-14-83	1B	Jim Gott	at Toronto
1374	4-14-83	1B	Roy Lee Jackson	at Toronto
1375	4-17-83	1B	Steve Renko	Kansas City
1376	4-17-83	1B	Steve Renko	Kansas City
1377	4-18-83	3B	Mike Brown	at Boston
1378	4-18-83	1B	Doug Bird	at Boston
1379	4-18-83	1B	Luis Aponte	at Boston
1380	4-20-83	1B	Dennis Eckersley	at Boston
1381	4-22-83	1B	Danny Darwin	at Texas
1382	4-23-83	1B	Rick Honeycutt	at Texas
1383	4-23-83	1B	Rick Honeycutt	at Texas
1384	4-23-83	1B	Rick Honeycutt	at Texas
1385	4-24-83	2B	Charlie Hough	at Texas
1386	4-26-83	2B	Lamarr Hoyt	Chicago
1387	4-27-83	2B	Floyd Bannister	Chicago
1388	4-27-83	1B	Floyd Bannister	Chicago
1389	4-29-83	1B	Brad Havens	at Minnesota
1390	4-29-83	1B	Brad Havens	at Minnesota
1391	4-30-83	1B	Rick Lysander	at Minnesota
1392	4-30-83	1B	Ron Davis	at Minnesota
1393	5-01-83	2B	Frank Viola	at Minnesota
1394	5-01-83	HR-3	Al Williams	at Minnesota
1395	5-02-83	1B	Lamarr Hoyt	at Chicago
1396	5-03-83	HR-2	Jerry Koosman	at Chicago
1397	5-04-83	1B	Dennis Lamp	at Chicago
1398	5-08-83	1B	Mike Smithson	Texas
1399	5-08-83	HR-3	Odell Jones	Texas
1400	5-10-83	1B	Brad Havens	Minnesota
1401	5-10-83	1B	Rick Lysander	Minnesota
1402	5-11-83	2B	Al Williams	Minnesota
1403	5-12-83	HR-1	Mike Brown	Boston
1404	5-12-83	1B	Bob Stanley	Boston
1405	5-15-83	1B	Bob Ojeda	Boston
1406	5-16-83	1B	Dave Stieb	Toronto
1407	5-17-83	1B	Jim Clancy	Toronto
1408	5-17-83	1B	Jim Acker	Toronto
1409	5-18-83	2B	Luis Leal	Toronto
1410	5-18-83	1B	Luis Leal	Toronto
1411	5-18-83	1B	Roy Lee Jackson	Toronto
1412	5-20-83	2B	Jim Beattie	at Seattle
1413	5-22-83	1B	Ed Vandeberg	at Seattle
1414	5-23-83	1B	Bill Krueger	at Oakland
1415	5-24-83	1B	Tim Conroy	at Oakland
1416	5-24-83	1B	Matt Keough	at Oakland
1417	5-25-83	3B	Tom Underwood	at Oakland
1418	5-27-83	1B	Gaylord Perry	Seattle
1419	5-27-83	1B	Bill Caudill	Seattle
1420	5-28-83	1B	Bob Stoddard	Seattle
1421	5-29-83	1B	Matt Young	Seattle
1422	5-29-83	2B	Matt Young	Seattle
1423	5-31-83	2B	Tim Conroy	Oakland

HIT	DATE	TYPE	PITCHER	OPPONENT
1424	6-01-83	1B	Tom Burgmeier	Oakland
1425	6-02-83	2B	Chris Codiroli	Oakland
1426	6-02-83	HR-2	Chris Codiroli	Oakland
1427	6-05-83	1B	Luis Sanchez	California
1428	6-06-83	2B	Dave Goltz	California
1429	6-07-83	1B	Dennis Martinez	at Baltimore
1430	6-09-83	3B	Mike Boddicker	at Baltimore
1431	6-11-83	2B	Ron Guidry	New York
1432	6-12-83	1B	George Frazier	New York
1433	6-13-83	1B	Allan Ramirez	Baltimore
1434	6-13-83	1B	Tippy Martinez	Baltimore
1435	6-15-83	1B	Storm Davis	Baltimore
1436	6-15-83	1B	Storm Davis	Baltimore
1437	6-15-83	2B	Tippy Martinez	Baltimore
1438	6-16-83	1B	Scott McGregor	Baltimore
1439	6-17-83	HR-1	Dave Righetti	at New York
1440	6-18-83	1B	Jay Howell	at New York
1441	6-18-83	2B	Jay Howell	at New York
1442	6-19-83	1B	Matt Keough	at New York
1443	6-19-83	1B	Matt Keough	at New York
1444	6-21-83	2B	Juan Berenguer	at Detroit
1445	6-22-83	HR-1	Jack Morris	at Detroit
1446	6-22-83	1B	Jack Morris	at Detroit
1447	6-24-83	1B	Lary Sorsensen	Cleveland
1448	6-25-83	2B	Juan Eichelberger	Cleveland
1449	6-25-83	1B	Dan Spillner	Cleveland
1450	6-26-83	2B	Bert Blyleven	Cleveland
1451	6-28-83	2B	Dan Petry	Detroit
1452	7-01-83	1B	Juan Eichelberger	at Cleveland
1453	7-01-83	HR-1	Lary Sorensen	at Cleveland
1454	7-02-83	1B	Bert Blyleven	at Cleveland
1455	7-04-83	1B	Len Barker	at Cleveland
1456	7-08-83	HR-1	Lamarr Hoyt	at Chicago
1457	7-09-83	1B	Jerry Koosman	at Chicago
1458	7-10-83	2B	Kevin Hickey	at Chicago
1459	7-10-83	3B	Dick Tidrow	at Chicago
1460	7-14-83	1B	Al Williams	Minnesota
1461	7-16-83	1B	Frank Viola	Minnesota
1462	7-16-83	HR-1	Rick Lysander	Minnesota
1463	7-17-83	1B	Ken Schrom	Minnesota
1464	7-17-83	2B	Brad Havens	Minnesota
1465	7-18-83	2B	Danny Darwin	Texas(1)
1466	7-18-83	2B	Danny Darwin	Texas(1)
1467	7-18-83	1B	Danny Darwin	Texas(1)
1468	7-20-83	1B	Mike Smithson	Texas
1469	7-21-83	2B	Britt Burns	Chicago
1470	7-21-83	1B	Britt Burns	Chicago
1471	7-21-83	2B	Britt Burns	Chicago
1472	7-21-83	2B	Salome Barojas	Chicago
1473	7-22-83	1B	Dennis Lamp	Chicago
1474	7-24-83	2B	Jerry Koosman	Chicago
1475	7-29-83	1B	Dennis Eckersley	at Boston
1476	7-29-83	2B	Dennis Eckersley	at Boston
1477	7-30-83	2B	John Tudor	at Boston
1478	7-31-83	1B	Bob Stanley	at Boston
1479	8-02-83	2B	Larry Gura	Kansas City(2)
1480	8-08-83	1B	Larry Gura	at K. C.(1)
1481	8-08-83	1B	Larry Gura	at K. C.(1)
1482	8-08-83	3B	Dan Quisenberry	at K. C.(1)

HIT	DATE	TYPE	PITCHER	OPPONENT
1483	8-09-83	1B	Bud Black	at Kansas City
1484	8-10-83	1B	Paul Splittorff	at Kansas City
1485	8-10-83	2B	Paul Splittorff	at Kansas City
1486	8-11-83	1B	Doyle Alexander	at Toronto
1487	8-11-83	3B	Doyle Alexander	at Toronto
1488	8-13-83	1B	Jim Clancy	at Toronto
1489	8-13-83	2B	Jim Clancy	at Toronto
1490	8-16-83	1B	Doug Bird	Boston
1491	8-16-83	1B	Doug Bird	Boston
1492	8-17-83	2B	Bob Ojeda	Boston(1)
1493	8-17-83	1B	Bob Ojeda	Boston(1)
1494	8-20-83	1B	Steve McCatty	Oakland
1495	8-20-83	1B	Steve McCatty	Oakland
1496	8-22-83	HR-1	Bob Stoddard	Seattle
1497	8-23-83	1B	Mike Moore	Seattle
1498	8-24-83	1B	John Curtis	California
1499	8-24-83	1B	Andy Hassler	California
1500	8-25-83	2B	Tommy John	California
1501	8-28-83	1B	Mike Warren	at Oakland
1502	8-28-83	1B	Keith Atherton	at Oakland
1503	8-29-83	1B	Bryan Clark	at Seattle
1504	8-29-83	1B	Bryan Clark	at Seattle
1505	8-29-83	1B	Bryan Clark	at Seattle
1506	8-31-83	1B	Bob Stoddard	at Seattle
1507	9-02-83	1B	Ken Forsch	at California
1508	9-02-83	2B	Ricky Steirer	at California
1509	9-05-83	3B	Shane Rawley	New York
1510	9-06-83	1B	Dave Righetti	New York
1511	9-07-83	1B	Ray Fontenot	New York
1512	9-08-83	1B	George Frazier	New York
1513	9-09-83	1B	Jack Morris	Detroit(1)
1514	9-09-83	1B	Jack Morris	Detroit(1)
1515	9-09-83	1B	Dave Gumpert	Detroit(2)
1516	9-11-83	1B	Dan Petry	Detroit
1517	9-12-83	1B	George Frazier	at New York
1518	9-16-83	HR-1	Mike Boddicker	at Baltimore
1519	9-18-83	1B	Jim Palmer	at Baltimore
1520	9-18-83	2B	Jim Palmer	at Baltimore
1521	9-18-83	1B	Tim Stoddard	at Baltimore
1522	9-19-83	3B	Scott McGregor	at Baltimore
1523	9-20-83	1B	Rick Sutcliffe	at Cleveland
1524	9-20-83	1B	Bud Anderson	at Cleveland
1525	9-20-83	2B	Dan Spillner	at Cleveland
1526	9-21-83	2B	Neal Heaton	at Cleveland
1527	9-22-83	1B	Lary Sorensen	at Cleveland
1528	9-22-83	1B	Lary Sorensen	at Cleveland
1529	9-23-83	2B	Scott McGregor	Baltimore
1530	9-24-83	2B	Dennis Martinez	Baltimore
1531	9-24-83	1B	Jim Palmer	Baltimore
1532	9-24-83	2B	Jim Palmer	Baltimore
1533	9-25-83	1B	Storm Davis	Baltimore
1534	9-27-83	1B	Lary Sorensen	Cleveland
1535	9-27-83	3B	Lary Sorensen	Cleveland
1536	9-27-83	1B	Mike Jeffcoat	Cleveland
1537	9-28-83	HR-2	Jamie Easterly	Cleveland
1538	9-29-83	2B	Rick Sutcliffe	Cleveland
1539	9-29-83	1B	Rick Sutcliffe	Cleveland
1540	9-30-83	1B	Juan Berenguer	at Detroit
1541	9-30-83	HR-1	Juan Berenguer	at Detroit

"I'm obviously very happy here. I have no desire to go anywhere else."

— Robin Yount, 1983

BREWERS

YOUNT
1984

HIT	DATE	TYPE	PITCHER	OPPONENT
1542	4-04-84	1B	Ray Burris	at Oakland
1543	4-06-84	1B	Mike Stanton	at Seattle
1544	4-10-84	HR-2	John Curtis	at California
1545	4-11-84	1B	Ron Romanick	at California
1546	4-11-84	1B	Ron Romanick	at California
1547	4-11-84	1B	Luis Sanchez	at California
1548	4-13-84	1B	Bud Black	at Kansas City
1549	4-13-84	2B	Bud Black	at Kansas City
1550	4-14-84	1B	Mark Gubicza	at Kansas City
1551	4-14-84	1B	Joe Beckwith	at Kansas City
1552	4-17-84	1B	Tom Seaver	Chicago
1553	4-19-84	1B	Rich Dotson	Chicago
1554	4-20-84	1B	Jim Beattie	Seattle
1555	4-24-84	1B	Lary Sorensen	Oakland
1556	4-26-84	1B	Tommy John	California
1557	4-28-84	1B	Jose Rijo	at New York
1558	4-28-84	3B	Bob Shirley	at New York
1559	4-28-84	1B	Bob Shirley	at New York
1560	4-29-84	2B	Phil Niekro	at New York
1561	5-01-84	1B	Larry Gura	Kansas City
1562	5-04-84	1B	Phil Niekro	New York
1563	5-04-84	2B	Phil Niekro	New York
1564	5-05-84	1B	Dave Righetti	New York
1565	5-05-84	1B	Curt Brown	New York
1566	5-06-84	1B	Ray Fontenot	New York
1567	5-07-84	1B	Lamarr Hoyt	at Chicago
1568	5-07-84	1B	Lamarr Hoyt	at Chicago
1569	5-07-84	1B	Britt Burns	at Chicago
1570	5-08-84	1B	Salome Barojas	at Chicago
1571	5-08-84	2B	Britt Burns	at Chicago
1572	5-08-84	1B	Juan Agosto	at Chicago
1573	5-09-84	HR-1	Tom Seaver	at Chicago
1574	5-11-84	1B	Ed Hodge	Minnesota
1575	5-11-84	HR-2	Ed Hodge	Minnesota
1576	5-11-84	1B	Larry Pashnick	Minnesota
1577	5-13-84	1B	Frank Viola	Minnesota
1578	5-14-84	1B	Mike Mason	Texas
1579	5-16-84	1B	Danny Darwin	Texas
1580	5-16-84	1B	Danny Darwin	Texas
1581	5-17-84	1B	Frank Tanana	Texas
1582	5-18-84	1B	Rick Sutcliffe	Cleveland
1583	5-18-84	1B	Mike Jeffcoat	Cleveland
1584	5-19-84	2B	Dan Spillner	Cleveland
1585	5-19-84	2B	George Frazier	Cleveland
1586	5-20-84	1B	Neal Heaton	Cleveland
1587	5-20-84	1B	Neal Heaton	Cleveland
1588	5-22-84	1B	Danny Darwin	at Texas
1589	5-22-84	1B	Danny Darwin	at Texas
1590	5-22-84	1B	Jim Bibby	at Texas
1591	5-23-84	1B	Frank Tanana	at Texas
1592	5-24-84	1B	Dave Stewart	at Texas
1593	5-25-84	1B	John Butcher	at Minnesota
1594	5-25-84	2B	John Butcher	at Minnesota
1595	5-26-84	3B	Ed Hodge	at Minnesota
1596	5-26-84	1B	Pete Filson	at Minnesota
1597	5-27-84	1B	Len Whitehouse	at Minnesota
1598	5-20-84	1B	Steve Farr	at Cleveland(2)
1599	5-30-84	1B	Steve Farr	at Cleveland(2)
1600	6-02-84	HR-1	Roger Clemens	Boston
1601	6-02-84	HR-2	Roger Clemens	Boston
1602	6-02-84	2B	Dennis Boyd	Boston
1603	6-05-84	1B	Tom Underwood	at Baltimore
1604	6-05-84	1B	Sammy Stewart	at Baltimore
1605	6-07-84	1B	Roger Clemens	at Boston
1606	6-07-84	1B	Steve Crawford	at Boston
1607	6-07-84	1B	Steve Crawford	at Boston
1608	6-09-84	1B	Bob Ojeda	at Boston
1609	6-10-84	1B	Al Nipper	at Boston
1610	6-10-84	1B	Rich Gale	at Boston
1611	6-12-84	2B	Storm Davis	Baltimore
1612	6-12-84	1B	Storm Davis	Baltimore
1613	6-13-84	2B	Mike Flanagan	Baltimore
1614	6-13-84	2B	Mike Flanagan	Baltimore
1615	6-13-84	2B	Mike Flanagan	Baltimore
1616	6-13-84	1B	Bill Swaggerty	Baltimore
1617	6-14-84	1B	Dennis Martinez	Baltimore
1618	6-16-84	1B	Juan Berenguer	Detroit
1619	6-16-84	1B	Juan Berenguer	Detroit
1620	6-17-84	1B	Dave Rozema	Detroit
1621	6-19-84	1B	Dave Stieb	at Toronto
1622	6-19-84	1B	Jim Acker	at Toronto
1623	6-19-84	2B	Jimmy Key	at Toronto
1624	6-20-84	2B	Doyle Alexander	at Toronto
1625	6-25-84	1B	Jim Acker	Toronto(2)
1626	6-25-84	1B	Bryan Clark	Toronto(2)
1627	6-26-84	HR-2	Luis Leal	Toronto
1628	6-27-84	1B	Jim Clancy	Toronto
1629	6-27-84	2B	Roy Lee Jackson	Toronto
1630	6-28-84	1B	Tommy John	California
1631	7-02-84	2B	Mike Moore	Seattle(1)
1632	7-02-84	1B	Mike Moore	Seattle(1)
1633	7-02-84	1B	Dave Geisel	Seattle(2)
1634	7-03-84	1B	Edwin Nunez	Seattle
1635	7-04-84	2B	Ed Vande Berg	Seattle
1636	7-05-84	1B	Bill Krueger	Oakland
1637	7-05-84	1B	Lary Sorensen	Oakland
1638	7-06-84	HR-2	Ray Burris	Oakland(1)
1639	7-06-84	1B	Curt Young	Oakland(2)
1640	7-07-84	3B	Steve McCatty	Oakland
1641	7-08-84	1B	Lary Sorensen	Oakland
1642	7-13-84	HR-2	Geoff Zahn	at California
1643	7-13-84	1B	Geoff Zahn	at California
1644	7-13-84	1B	Geoff Zahn	at California
1645	7-15-84	1B	Tommy John	at California
1646	7-15-84	1B	Luis Sanchez	at California
1647	7-18-84	1B	Mike Moore	at Seattle
1648	7-19-84	2B	Bill Caudill	at Oakland
1649	7-20-84	1B	Bill Caudill	at Oakland
1650	7-21-84	1B	Lary Sorensen	at Oakland
1651	7-21-84	3B	Lary Sorensen	at Oakland
1652	7-21-84	1B	Chuck Rainey	at Oakland
1653	7-27-84	1B	Larry Gura	Kansas City(1)
1654	7-27-84	1B	Joe Beckwith	Kansas City(1)
1655	7-29-84	1B	Mark Gubicza	Kansas City
1656	7-30-84	2B	Dave Righetti	at New York
1657	7-31-84	1B	Ray Fontenot	at New York
1658	7-31-84	1B	Ray Fontenot	at New York
1659	7-31-84	2B	Ray Fontenot	at New York
1660	8-02-84	1B	Jay Howell	at New York
1661	8-04-84	2B	Tom Seaver	Chicago
1662	8-05-84	1B	Richard Dotson	Chicago
1663	8-07-84	HR-2	Larry Gura	at Kansas City
1664	8-07-84	HR-2	Larry Gura	at Kansas City
1665	8-09-84	1B	Mark Gubicza	at Kansas City
1666	8-10-84	1B	Richard Dotson	at Chicago
1667	8-11-84	1B	Dan Spillner	at Chicago
1668	8-12-84	1B	Ron Reed	at Chicago
1669	8-13-84	1B	John Butcher	at Minnesota
1670	8-14-84	1B	Ed Hodge	at Minnesota
1671	8-15-84	1B	Ken Schrom	at Minnesota
1672	8-15-84	2B	Len Whitehouse	at Minnesota
1673	8-17-84	1B	Bert Blyleven	at Cleveland
1674	8-19-84	1B	Neal Heaton	at Cleveland(1)
1675	8-19-84	1B	Neal Heaton	at Cleveland(1)
1676	8-19-84	HR-1	Ernie Camacho	at Cleveland(2)
1677	8-23-84	1B	Frank Viola	Minnesota
1678	8-23-84	1B	Frank Viola	Minnesota
1679	8-24-84	1B	Frank Tanana	Texas
1680	8-24-84	1B	Frank Tanana	Texas
1681	8-25-84	2B	Charlie Hough	Texas
1682	8-26-84	1B	Mike Mason	Texas
1683	8-26-84	1B	Tom Henke	Texas
1684	8-27-84	1B	Bert Blyleven	Cleveland
1685	8-28-84	3B	Neal Heaton	Cleveland
1686	8-29-84	1B	Steve Comer	Cleveland
1687	8-29-84	1B	Steve Farr	Cleveland
1688	8-30-84	1B	Don Schulze	Cleveland
1689	8-30-84	1B	Don Schulze	Cleveland
1690	8-30-84	1B	Jamie Easterly	Cleveland
1691	8-31-84	1B	Dickie Noles	at Texas
1692	9-01-84	1B	Tom Henke	at Texas
1693	9-04-84	1B	Al Nipper	Boston
1694	9-05-84	1B	John H. Johnson	Boston
1695	9-08-84	1B	Storm Davis	at Baltimore
1696	9-08-84	1B	Storm Davis	at Baltimore
1697	9-10-84	1B	Mike Brown	at Boston
1698	9-10-84	2B	Mike Brown	at Boston
1699	9-11-84	1B	Dennis Boyd	at Boston
1700	9-11-84	1B	Dennis Boyd	at Boston
1701	9-11-84	HR-1	Steve Crawford	at Boston
1702	9-14-84	2B	Mike Boddicker	Baltimore
1703	9-14-84	3B	Mike Boddicker	Baltimore
1704	9-15-84	2B	Mike Flanagan	Baltimore
1705	9-15-84	HR-4	Sammy Stewart	Baltimore
1706	9-16-84	1B	Storm Davis	Baltimore
1707	9-16-84	1B	Sammy Stewart	Baltimore
1708	9-17-84	HR-1	Aurelio Lopez	at Detroit
1709	9-18-84	1B	Randy O'Neal	at Detroit
1710	9-18-84	1B	Willie Hernandez	at Detroit
1711	9-19-84	1B	Jack Morris	at Detroit
1712	9-19-84	1B	Willie Hernandez	at Detroit
1713	9-20-84	1B	Dave Stieb	at Toronto
1714	9-21-84	1B	Jim Gott	at Toronto
1715	9-22-84	1B	Doyle Alexander	at Toronto
1716	9-24-84	HR-2	Doug Bair	Detroit
1717	9-26-84	1B	Bill Scherrer	Detroit
1718	9-26-84	1B	Aurelio Lopez	Detroit
1719	9-28-84	1B	Jim Clancy	Toronto
1720	9-28-84	1B	Jim Clancy	Toronto
1721	9-28-84	1B	Jeff Musselmann	Toronto
1722	9-29-84	1B	Dave Stieb	Toronto
1723	9-29-84	1B	Dave Stieb	Toronto
1724	9-29-84	1B	Dave Stieb	Toronto
1725	9-29-84	HR-1	Dave Stieb	Toronto
1726	9-30-84	2B	Doyle Alexander	Toronto
1727	9-30-84	3B	Doyle Alexander	Toronto

"I don't get goose bumps when I open my pay envelope. But look at me when I start talking about 1982." — *Robin Yount, 1984*

ROBIN
1985

HIT	DATE	TYPE	PITCHER	OPPONENT
1728	4-11-85	1B	Tim Lollar	Chicago
1729	4-12-85	1B	Dave Schmidt	at Texas
1730	4-13-85	1B	Charlie Hough	at Texas
1731	4-13-85	1B	Charlie Hough	at Texas
1732	4-14-85	1B	Dave Rozema	at Texas
1733	4-14-85	1B	Greg Harris	at Texas
1734	4-17-85	1B	Jack Morris	at Detroit
1735	4-21-85	1B	Mike Mason	Texas
1736	4-22-85	1B	Richard Dotson	at Chicago
1737	4-23-85	1B	Floyd Bannister	at Chicago
1738	4-23-85	1B	Floyd Bannister	at Chicago
1739	4-24-85	2B	Britt Burns	at Chicago
1740	4-24-85	1B	Dan Spillner	at Chicago
1741	4-25-85	1B	Bill Scherrer	Detroit
1742	4-27-85	2B	Dan Petry	Detroit
1743	4-27-85	2B	Dan Petry	Detroit
1744	4-27-85	1B	Dan Petry	Detroit
1745	4-29-85	1B	Mike Moore	at Seattle
1746	4-30-85	3B	Mark Langston	at Seattle
1747	5-01-85	1B	Steve McCatty	at Oakland
1748	5-01-85	HR-2	Tom Conroy	at Oakland
1749	5-07-85	1B	Jim Beattie	Seattle
1750	5-07-85	1B	Jim Beattie	Seattle
1751	5-08-85	1B	Mike Moore	Seattle
1752	5-10-85	1B	Ron Romanick	California
1753	5-10-85	HR-2	Ron Romanick	California
1754	5-12-85	HR-1	Doug Corbett	California
1755	5-14-85	1B	Chris Codiroli	Oakland
1756	5-15-85	1B	Bill Krueger	Oakland
1757	5-17-85	1B	Bret Saberhagen	Kansas City
1758	5-19-85	1B	Mark Gubicza	Kansas City
1759	5-19-85	1B	Mike Jones	Kansas City
1760	5-19-85	HR-1	Mike LaCoss	Kansas City
1761	5-21-85	1B	Keith Creel	at Cleveland
1762	5-22-85	2B	Bert Blyleven	at Cleveland
1763	5-22-85	1B	Jamie Easterly	at Cleveland
1764	5-24-85	1B	Mike Smithson	Minnesota
1765	5-25-85	HR-2	Pete Filson	Minnesota
1766	5-26-85	HR-2	John Butcher	Minnesota
1767	5-28-85	3B	Neal Heaton	Cleveland
1768	5-29-85	1B	Don Schulze	Cleveland
1769	5-29-85	1B	Rich Thompson	Cleveland
1770	5-31-85	1B	Pete Filson	at Minnesota
1771	5-31-85	1B	Pete Filson	at Minnesota
1772	6-01-85	2B	John Butcher	at Minnesota
1773	6-05-85	1B	Bud Black	at Kansas City
1774	6-05-85	1B	Mike Jones	at Kansas City
1775	6-06-85	1B	Ed Whitson	New York
1776	6-06-85	2B	Ed Whitson	New York
1777	6-07-85	2B	Ron Guidry	New York
1778	6-08-85	1B	Dennis Rasmussen	New York
1779	6-09-85	2B	Phil Niekro	New York
1780	6-09-85	1B	Phil Niekro	New York
1781	6-11-85	1B	Roger Clemens	at Boston
1782	6-11-85	1B	Roger Clemens	at Boston
1783	6-12-85	2B	Al Nipper	at Boston
1784	6-13-85	1B	Scott McGregor	at Baltimore
1785	6-15-85	1B	Ken Dixon	at Baltimore
1786	6-16-85	1B	Mike Boddicker	at Baltimore
1787	6-17-85	1B	Dave Stieb	Toronto
1788	6-18-85	1B	Luis Leal	Toronto
1789	6-21-85	1B	Mike Boddicker	Baltimore
1790	6-21-85	1B	Tippy Martinez	Baltimore
1791	6-22-85	1B	Scott McGregor	Baltimore
1792	6-23-85	2B	Storm Davis	Baltimore
1793	6-26-85	2B	Doyle Alexander	at Toronto
1794	6-27-85	1B	Jimmy Key	at Toronto
1795	6-28-85	2B	Ron Guidry	at New York
1796	6-28-85	1B	Ron Guidry	at New York
1797	6-28-85	1B	Brian Fisher	at New York
1798	6-29-85	1B	Phil Niekro	at New York
1799	6-29-85	1B	Dennis Rasmussen	at New York
1800	7-01-85	1B	Mike Trujillo	Boston
1801	7-03-85	1B	Bruce Hurst	Boston
1802	7-03-85	2B	Bruce Hurst	Boston
1803	7-05-85	1B	Edwin Nunez	at Seattle
1804	7-06-85	1B	Frank Wills	at Seattle
1805	7-07-85	2B	Bill Swift	at Seattle
1806	7-08-85	1B	Mike Witt	at California
1807	7-11-85	1B	Steve Ontiveros	at Oakland
1808	7-12-85	1B	Chris Codiroli	at Oakland
1809	7-12-85	HR-1	Jay Howell	at Oakland
1810	7-13-85	1B	Tim Birtsas	at Oakland
1811	7-14-85	1B	Bill Krueger	at Oakland
1812	7-14-85	1B	Keith Atherton	at Oakland
1813	7-18-85	1B	Mike Moore	Seattle
1814	7-18-85	HR-1	Mike Moore	Seattle
1815	7-18-85	1B	Mike Moore	Seattle
1816	7-19-85	1B	Matt Young	Seattle
1817	7-19-85	1B	Matt Young	Seattle
1818	7-19-85	1B	Roy Thomas	Seattle
1819	7-20-85	2B	Bill Swift	Seattle
1820	7-20-85	1B	Salome Barojas	Seattle
1821	7-20-85	1B	Roy Thomas	Seattle
1822	7-21-85	HR-2	Frank Wills	Seattle
1823	7-22-85	2B	Doug Corbett	California
1824	7-24-85	2B	Ron Romanick	California
1825	7-24-85	1B	Ron Romanick	California
1826	7-25-85	1B	Tim Birtsas	Oakland
1827	7-25-85	2B	Tim Birtsas	Oakland
1828	7-29-85	HR-1	Charlie Hough	Texas
1829	7-30-85	2B	Burt Hooton	Texas
1830	7-30-85	2B	Burt Hooton	Texas
1831	7-30-85	2B	Dave Rozema	Texas
1832	7-31-85	1B	Mike Mason	Texas
1833	8-04-85	2B	Aurelio Lopez	at Detroit(1)
1834	8-04-85	3B	Juan Berenguer	at Detroit(2)
1835	8-09-85	HR-1	Tom Seaver	at Chicago
1836	8-10-85	HR-1	Floyd Bannister	at Chicago
1837	8-10-85	1B	Floyd Bannister	at Chicago
1838	8-11-85	1B	Joel Davis	at Chicago
1839	8-12-85	2B	Frank Tanana	Detroit
1840	8-12-85	1B	Frank Tanana	Detroit
1841	8-15-85	HR-2	Floyd Bannister	Chicago
1842	8-16-85	2B	Dave Wehrmeister	Chicago
1843	8-17-85	HR-1	Gene Nelson	Chicago
1844	8-17-85	HR-2	Dan Spillner	Chicago
1845	8-20-85	1B	John Butcher	Minnesota
1846	8-21-85	1B	Bert Blyleven	Minnesota
1847	8-21-85	1B	Ron Davis	Minnesota
1848	8-26-85	2B	Roy Smith	at Cleveland(2)
1849	8-26-85	1B	Roy Smith	at Cleveland
1850	8-27-85	1B	Danny Jackson	Kansas City
1851	8-27-85	2B	Danny Jackson	Kansas City
1852	8-30-85	1B	Vern Ruhle	Cleveland
1853	8-31-85	1B	Neal Heaton	Cleveland
1854	8-31-85	1B	Neal Heaton	Cleveland
1855	8-31-85	1B	Jerry Reed	Cleveland
1856	9-01-85	1B	Dave Von Ohlen	Cleveland

"I have no desire to go back and play shortstop. I've pretty much conceded those days are over." — *Robin Yount, 1985*

2000
1986

HIT	DATE	TYPE	PITCHER	OPPONENT
1857	4-07-86	1B	Tom Seaver	at Chicago
1858	4-09-86	1B	Richard Dotson	at Chicago
1859	4-09-86	1B	Richard Dotson	at Chicago
1860	4-09-86	1B	Gene Nelson	at Chicago
1861	4-09-86	1B	Bob James	at Chicago
1862	4-10-86	1B	Joel Davis	at Chicago
1863	4-10-86	2B	Dave Schmidt	at Chicago
1864	4-10-86	1B	Bob James	at Chicago
1865	4-11-86	1B	Bob Tewksbury	at New York
1866	4-11-86	2B	Bob Tewksbury	at New York
1867	4-11-86	1B	Bob Tewksbury	at New York
1868	4-13-86	1B	Ron Guidry	at New York
1869	4-13-86	HR-1	Bob Shirley	at New York
1870	4-14-86	1B	Ed Correa	Texas
1871	4-18-86	1B	Brian Fisher	New York
1872	4-19-86	1B	Ron Guidry	New York
1873	4-19-86	1B	Dave Righetti	New York
1874	4-23-86	1B	Tom Seaver	Chicago
1875	4-23-86	1B	Tom Seaver	Chicago
1876	4-25-86	1B	Jose Guzman	at Texas
1877	4-25-86	1B	Jose Guzman	at Texas
1878	4-25-86	2B	Dwayne Henry	at Texas
1879	4-26-86	1B	Ed Correa	at Texas
1880	4-26-86	1B	Ed Correa	at Texas
1881	4-26-86	1B	Mitch Williams	at Texas
1882	4-27-86	2B	Greg Harris	at Texas
1883	4-29-86	1B	Chris Codiroli	Oakland
1884	4-30-86	1B	Jose Rijo	Oakland
1885	4-30-86	3B	Keith Atherton	Oakland
1886	5-01-86	2B	Moose Haas	Oakland
1887	5-02-86	1B	Don Sutton	Oakland
1888	5-04-86	1B	Kirk McCaskill	California
1889	5-06-86	1B	Bill Swift	Seattle
1890	5-06-86	1B	Bill Swift	Seattle
1891	5-06-86	1B	Jerry Reed	Seattle
1892	5-06-86	1B	Karl Best	Seattle
1893	5-07-86	1B	Joaquin Andujar	at Oakland
1894	5-07-86	1B	Bill Mooneyham	at Oakland
1895	5-09-86	1B	Kirk McCaskill	at California
1896	5-10-86	1B	Mike Witt	at California
1897	5-10-86	1B	Mike Witt	at California
1898	5-11-86	2B	Jim Slaton	at California
1899	5-11-86	1B	Jim Slaton	at California
1900	5-11-86	1B	Doug Corbett	at California
1901	5-13-86	1B	Mike Morgan	at Seattle
1902	5-13-86	2B	Pete Ladd	at Seattle
1903	5-16-86	2B	Mike Smithson	Minnesota
1904	5-16-86	1B	Mike Smithson	Minnesota
1905	5-16-86	1B	Juan Agosto	Minnesota
1906	5-17-86	1B	Mark Portugal	Minnesota
1907	5-17-86	HR-1	Mark Portugal	Minnesota
1908	5-18-86	2B	Bert Blyleven	Minnesota
1909	6-03-86	1B	Bret Saberhagen	Kansas City
1910	6-04-86	3B	Dennis Leonard	Kansas City
1911	6-05-86	1B	Jeff Sellers	Boston

HIT	DATE	TYPE	PITCHER	OPPONENT
1912	6-06-86	1B	Roger Clemens	Boston
1913	6-07-86	2B	Dennis Boyd	Boston
1914	6-08-86	2B	Mike Brown	Boston
1915	6-08-86	2B	Sammy Stewart	Boston
1916	6-09-86	1B	Storm Davis	Baltimore
1917	6-09-86	1B	Storm Davis	Baltimore
1918	6-11-86	1B	Don Aase	Baltimore
1919	6-13-86	1B	Dennis Boyd	at Boston
1920	6-15-86	HR-2	Jeff Sellers	at Boston
1921	6-15-86	2B	Jeff Sellers	at Boston
1922	6-16-86	1B	Doyle Alexander	Toronto
1923	6-16-86	2B	Doyle Alexander	Toronto
1924	6-16-86	1B	Doyle Alexander	Toronto
1925	6-16-86	1B	Don Gordon	Toronto
1926	6-21-86	1B	Frank Tanana	Detroit
1927	6-22-86	1B	Randy O'Neal	Detroit
1928	6-22-86	1B	Randy O'Neal	Detroit
1929	6-23-86	1B	Dave Stieb	at Toronto
1930	6-23-86	2B	Dave Stieb	at Toronto
1931	6-23-86	1B	Jim Acker	at Toronto
1932	6-24-86	2B	John Cerutti	at Toronto
1933	6-25-86	2B	Jim Clancy	at Toronto
1934	6-30-86	1B	Scott McGregor	at Baltimore
1935	6-30-86	1B	Don Aase	at Baltimore
1936	7-01-86	1B	Mike Flanagan	at Baltimore
1937	7-01-86	1B	Mike Flanagan	at Baltimore
1938	7-04-86	1B	Doug Bair	Oakland
1939	7-07-86	1B	Mike Witt	California
1940	7-07-86	1B	Terry Forster	California
1941	7-08-86	1B	John Candelaria	California
1942	7-08-86	2B	Mike Cook	California
1943	7-09-86	1B	Don Sutton	California
1944	7-10-86	1B	Mark Langston	Seattle
1945	7-10-86	1B	Steve Fireovid	Seattle
1946	7-11-86	3B	Mike Morgan	Seattle
1947	7-19-86	1B	Moose Haas	at Oakland
1948	7-19-86	1B	Bill Mooneyham	at Oakland
1949	7-20-86	1B	Dave Von Ohlen	at Oakland(1)
1950	7-20-86	1B	Jose Rijo	at Oakland(2)
1951	7-21-86	1B	Ron Romanick	at California
1952	7-23-86	1B	Kirk McCaskill	at California
1953	7-25-86	2B	Mike Morgan	at Seattle
1954	7-26-86	1B	Jerry Reed	at Seattle
1955	7-27-86	2B	Mark Langston	at Seattle
1956	7-28-86	3B	Joe Niekro	New York
1957	7-28-86	3B	Joe Niekro	New York
1958	7-29-86	1B	Scott Nielsen	New York
1959	8-02-86	1B	Charlie Hough	Texas
1960	8-06-86	1B	Ron Guidry	at New York
1961	8-06-86	HR-1	Ron Guidry	at New York
1962	8-07-86	1B	Joe Niekro	at New York
1963	8-12-86	1B	Charlie Hough	at Texas
1964	8-12-86	1B	Jeff Russell	at Texas
1965	8-12-86	1B	Greg Harris	at Texas

HIT	DATE	TYPE	PITCHER	OPPONENT
1966	8-13-86	2B	Dale Mohorcic	at Texas
1967	8-15-86	1B	Richard Dotson	at Chicago
1968	8-16-86	1B	Floyd Bannister	at Chicago
1969	8-16-86	2B	Gene Nelson	at Chicago
1970	8-17-86	1B	Bobby Thigpen	at Chicago
1971	8-18-86	1B	Tom Candiotti	at Cleveland
1972	8-18-86	1B	Tom Candiotti	at Cleveland
1973	8-18-86	1B	Tom Candiotti	at Cleveland
1974	8-19-86	1B	Jose Roman	at Cleveland
1975	8-20-86	1B	Scott Bailes	at Cleveland
1976	8-20-86	1B	Rich Yett	at Cleveland
1977	8-22-86	1B	Danny Jackson	Kansas City
1978	8-23-86	2B	Mark Gubicza	Kansas City
1979	8-23-86	1B	Mark Gubicza	Kansas City
1980	8-23-86	1B	Steve Farr	Kansas City
1981	8-24-86	1B	Dennis Leonard	Kansas City
1982	8-24-86	2B	Dan Quisenberry	Kansas City
1983	8-26-86	1B	George Frazier	Minnesota
1984	8-27-86	1B	Neal Heaton	Minnesota
1985	8-27-86	1B	George Frazier	Minnesota
1986	8-28-86	1B	Bert Blyleven	Minnesota
1987	8-30-86	2B	Mark Gubicza	at Kansas City
1988	8-31-86	1B	Scott Bankhead	at Kansas City
1989	8-31-86	2B	Scott Bankhead	at Kansas City
1990	8-31-86	2B	Scott Bankhead	at Kansas City
1991	9-01-86	1B	Ray Fontenot	at Minnesota
1992	9-02-86	2B	Bert Blyleven	at Minnesota
1993	9-03-86	HR-1	Mike Smithson	at Minnesota
1994	9-03-86	1B	Mike Smithson	at Minnesota
1995	9-03-86	1B	Mike Smithson	at Minnesota
1996	9-04-86	1B	Scott Bailes	Cleveland
1997	9-04-86	1B	Scott Bailes	Cleveland
1998	9-04-86	1B	Rich Yett	Cleveland
1999	9-05-86	HR-1	Phil Niekro	Cleveland
2000	9-06-86	1B	Don Schulze	Cleveland
2001	9-07-86	HR-1	Ken Schrom	Cleveland
2002	9-10-86	1B	Walt Terrell	at Detroit
2003	9-12-86	1B	Jim Clancy	Toronto
2004	9-13-86	1B	Joe Johnson	Toronto
2005	9-14-86	1B	Dave Stieb	Toronto
2006	9-14-86	3B	Jeff Musselman	Toronto
2007	9-15-86	1B	John Cerutti	Toronto
2008	9-15-86	1B	John Cerutti	Toronto
2009	9-16-86	1B	Calvin Schiraldi	at Boston
2010	9-18-86	1B	Bruce Hurst	at Boston
2011	9-19-86	1B	Ken Dixon	at Baltimore
2012	9-25-86	2B	Ken Dixon	Baltimore
2013	9-25-86	2B	Nate Snell	Baltimore
2014	9-25-86	HR-2	Mike Kinnunen	Baltimore
2015	10-3-86	3B	Jim Clancy	at Toronto
2016	10-5-86	2B	Joe Johnson	at Toronto
2017	10-5-86	1B	Tom Henke	at Toronto
2018	10-5-86	HR-1	Dave Stieb	at Toronto
2019	10-5-86	1B	Dave Stieb	at Toronto

"Maybe I'm a singles hitter, again. But that's better than not playing at all."

— Robin Yount, 1986

BREWERS
19

YOUNT
1987

HIT	DATE	TYPE	PITCHER	OPPONENT
2020	4-06-87	1B	Bob Stanley	Boston
2021	4-06-87	2B	Bob Stanley	Boston
2022	4-08-87	1B	Al Nipper	Boston
2023	4-09-87	1B	Jeff Sellers	Boston
2024	4-09-87	1B	Jeff Sellers	Boston
2025	4-10-87	HR-2	Jose Guzman	at Texas
2026	4-10-87	1B	Mike Loynd	at Texas
2027	4-10-87	1B	Greg Harris	at Texas
2028	4-11-87	1B	Jose Guzman	at Texas
2029	4-11-87	2B	Jose Guzman	at Texas
2030	4-14-87	HR-1	Ken Dixon	at Baltimore
2031	4-14-87	1B	Ken Dixon	at Baltimore
2032	4-15-87	1B	Mike Flanagan	at Baltimore
2033	4-17-87	2B	Mike Mason	Texas
2034	4-17-87	1B	Dale Mahorcic	Texas
2035	4-18-87	1B	Dale Mohorcic	Texas
2036	4-19-87	1B	Jose Guzman	Texas
2037	4-20-87	1B	Bobby Thigpen	at Chicago
2038	4-21-87	1B	Joel Davis	at Chicago
2039	4-25-87	1B	Ken Dixon	Baltimore
2040	4-25-87	1B	Tony Arnold	Baltimore
2041	4-26-87	3B	Mike Flanagan	Baltimore
2042	4-28-87	1B	John Candelaria	at California
2043	4-28-87	1B	John Candelaria	at California
2044	5-01-87	1B	Bill Wilkinson	at Seattle
2045	5-03-87	1B	Mike Morgan	at Seattle
2046	5-03-87	1B	Mike Morgan	at Seattle
2047	5-05-87	2B	Don Sutton	California
2048	5-05-87	1B	Mike Moore	California
2049	5-06-87	3B	Mike Witt	California
2050	5-08-87	1B	Stan Clarke	Seattle
2051	5-08-87	1B	Edwin Nunez	Seattle
2052	5-09-87	1B	Mike Morgan	Seattle
2053	5-10-87	1B	Mike Moore	Seattle
2054	5-10-87	1B	Mike Moore	Seattle
2055	5-12-87	1B	Dave Stewart	Oakland
2056	5-12-87	HR-1	Dave Stewart	Oakland
2057	5-12-87	2B	Gene Nelson	Oakland
2058	5-13-87	1B	Curt Young	Oakland
2059	5-17-87	2B	Bud Black	at Kansas City
2060	5-17-87	1B	Bud Black	at Kansas City
2061	5-17-87	1B	Steve Farr	at Kansas City
2062	5-19-87	1B	Jose DeLeon	Chicago
2063	5-19-87	1B	Jose DeLeon	Chicago
2064	5-19-87	HR-1	Jose DeLeon	Chicago
2065	5-20-87	HR-1	Jim Winn	Chicago
2066	5-22-87	2B	Phil Niekro	Cleveland
2067	5-23-87	1B	Steve Carlton	Cleveland
2068	5-24-87	1B	Ken Schrom	Cleveland
2069	5-27-87	2B	Frank Viola	at Minnesota
2070	5-31-87	HR-1	Greg Swindell	at Cleveland
2071	6-01-87	1B	Charlie Liebrandt	Kansas City
2072	6-02-87	1B	Bud Black	Kansas City
2073	6-02-87	1B	Rick Anderson	Kansas City
2074	6-02-87	2B	Rick Anderson	Kansas City
2075	6-03-87	1B	Mark Gubicza	Kansas City
2076	6-03-87	1B	Mark Gubicza	Kansas City
2077	6-05-87	1B	Tommy John	New York
2078	6-06-87	2B	Charles Hudson	New York
2079	6-06-87	1B	Tim Stoddard	New York
2080	6-07-87	1B	Dennis Rasmussen	New York
2081	6-07-87	1B	Dennis Rasmussen	New York
2082	6-10-87	1B	Walt Terrell	at Detroit
2083	6-13-87	1B	Rick Rhoden	at New York
2084	6-17-87	1B	Mike Smithson	Minnesota
2085	6-17-87	HR-2	Les Straker	Minnesota
2086	6-17-87	1B	Juan Berenguer	Minnesota
2087	6-18-87	1B	Mark Eichhorn	at Toronto
2088	6-18-87	3B	Jose Nunez	at Toronto
2089	6-19-87	1B	John Cerutti	at Toronto
2090	6-19-87	1B	John Cerutti	at Toronto
2091	6-21-87	1B	Joe Johnson	at Toronto
2092	6-21-87	HR-2	Joe Johnson	at Toronto
2093	6-21-87	2B	Mark Eichhorn	at Toronto
2094	6-22-87	1B	Dennis Boyd	at Boston
2095	6-24-87	1B	Bob Stanley	at Boston
2096	6-26-87	2B	Jimmy Key	Toronto
2097	6-26-87	1B	Jimmy Key	Toronto
2098	6-26-87	1B	Tom Henke	Toronto
2099	6-28-87	1B	Dave Stieb	Toronto
2100	6-28-87	HR-2	Dave Stieb	Toronto
2101	6-28-87	1B	Mark Eichhorn	Toronto
2102	7-01-87	1B	Mike Henneman	Detroit
2103	7-02-87	1B	Mike Witt	at California
2104	7-02-87	1B	Mike Witt	at California
2105	7-04-87	HR-1	Don Sutton	at California
2106	7-04-87	1B	Don Sutton	at California
2107	7-05-87	1B	Jack Lazorko	at California
2108	7-05-87	2B	Greg Minton	at California
2109	7-06-87	1B	Mike Morgan	at Seattle
2110	7-06-87	1B	Bill Wilkinson	at Seattle
2111	7-07-87	1B	Lee Guetterman	at Seattle
2112	7-07-87	1B	Lee Guetterman	at Seattle
2113	7-09-87	3B	Gene Nelson	at Oakland
2114	7-10-87	2B	Dave Stewart	at Oakland
2115	7-11-87	HR-2	Joaquin Andujar	at Oakland
2116	7-12-87	1B	Steve Ontiveros	at Oakland
2117	7-12-87	1B	Jay Howell	at Oakland
2118	7-16-87	1B	Kirk McCaskill	California
2119	7-16-87	1B	Kirk McCaskill	California
2120	7-16-87	1B	DeWayne Buice	California
2121	7-17-87	2B	Chuck Finley	California
2122	7-19-87	3B	Jerry Reuss	California
2123	7-19-87	HR-2	Jerry Reuss	California
2124	7-20-87	1B	Roy Thomas	Seattle
2125	7-20-87	2B	Jerry Reed	Seattle
2126	7-20-87	3B	Jerry Reed	Seattle
2127	7-21-87	HR-3	Mike Moore	Seattle
2128	7-23-87	1B	Dave Leiper	Oakland
2129	7-24-87	1B	Steve Ontiveros	Oakland
2130	7-24-87	1B	Steve Ontiveros	Oakland
2131	7-24-87	2B	Steve Ontiveros	Oakland
2132	7-25-87	1B	Bill Caudill	Oakland
2133	7-26-87	1B	Dave Leiper	Oakland
2134	7-28-87	1B	Jose Guzman	at Texas
2135	7-28-87	HR-2	Jose Guzman	at Texas
2136	7-29-87	1B	Greg Harris	at Texas
2137	7-29-87	1B	Greg Harris	at Texas
2138	7-29-87	1B	Greg Harris	at Texas
2139	7-29-87	1B	Matt Williams	at Texas
2140	7-31-87	1B	Richard Dotson	Chicago
2141	7-31-87	HR-1	Richard Dotson	Chicago
2142	7-31-87	1B	Scott Nielson	Chicago
2143	8-04-87	1B	John Habyan	Baltimore
2144	8-05-87	1B	Eric Bell	Baltimore
2145	8-06-87	1B	Mike Flanagan	Baltimore
2146	8-06-87	3B	Mike Griffin	Baltimore
2147	8-06-87	1B	Tom Niedenfuer	Baltimore
2148	8-08-87	1B	Bill Long	at Chicago(1)
2149	8-08-87	2B	Floyd Bannister	at Chicago(2)
2150	8-08-87	1B	Floyd Bannister	at Chicago(2)
2151	8-08-87	1B	Jim Winn	at Chicago(2)
2152	8-09-87	2B	Neil Allen	at Chicago
2153	8-09-87	1B	Bill Long	at Chicago
2154	8-10-87	1B	Steve Howe	Texas
2155	8-11-87	1B	Greg Harris	Texas
2156	8-14-87	2B	Eric Bell	at Baltimore
2157	8-15-87	1B	Mike Flanagan	at Baltimore
2158	8-16-87	1B	Dave Schmidt	at Baltimore
2159	8-16-87	1B	Dave Schmidt	at Baltimore
2160	8-17-87	1B	Scott Bailes	at Cleveland
2161	8-17-87	1B	Don Gordon	at Cleveland
2162	8-18-87	1B	Doug Jones	at Cleveland
2163	8-18-87	1B	John Farrell	at Cleveland
2164	8-19-87	1B	Don Gordon	at Cleveland
2165	8-20-87	1B	Ed Vande Berg	at Cleveland
2166	8-21-87	1B	Danny Jackson	Kansas City
2167	8-21-87	1B	Danny Jackson	Kansas City
2168	8-22-87	HR-1	Bret Saberhagen	Kansas City
2169	8-23-87	1B	Charlie Liebrandt	Kansas City
2170	8-23-87	1B	Charlie Liebrandt	Kansas City
2171	8-25-87	1B	Jamie Easterly	Cleveland
2172	8-25-87	1B	Don Gordon	Cleveland
2173	8-25-87	1B	Ed Vande Berg	Cleveland
2174	8-27-87	1B	Darrell Akerfelds	Cleveland
2175	8-28-87	1B	Les Straker	Minnesota
2176	8-28-87	1B	Les Straker	Minnesota
2177	8-29-87	1B	Bert Blyleven	Minnesota
2178	9-01-87	1B	Bret Saberhagen	at Kansas City
2179	9-01-87	1B	Bret Saberhagen	at Kansas City
2180	9-03-87	1B	Mark Gubicza	at Kansas City
2181	9-03-87	2B	Gene Garber	at Kansas City
2182	9-08-87	3B	Dave Stieb	Toronto
2183	9-08-87	1B	Jose Nunez	Toronto
2184	9-09-87	1B	Jim Clancy	Toronto
2185	9-09-87	HR-1	Jim Clancy	Toronto
2186	9-09-87	1B	David Wells	Toronto
2187	9-11-87	1B	Mike Henneman	Detroit
2188	9-13-87	1B	Walt Terrell	Detroit
2189	9-14-87	1B	Bill Gullickson	at New York
2190	9-16-87	1B	Tommy John	at New York
2191	9-16-87	1B	Tommy John	at New York
2192	9-16-87	1B	Tim Stoddard	at New York
2193	9-19-87	2B	Doyle Alexander	at Detroit
2194	9-20-87	1B	Jack Morris	at Detroit
2195	9-20-87	HR-2	Jack Morris	at Detroit
2196	9-22-87	2B	Tommy John	New York(1)
2197	9-22-87	HR-2	Charles Hudson	New York(1)
2198	9-22-87	HR-3	Neil Allen	New York(2)
2199	9-22-87	1B	Neil Allen	New York(2)
2200	9-23-87	1B	Bill Gullickson	New York
2201	9-23-87	1B	Dave Righetti	New York
2202	9-24-87	2B	Jeff Sellers	Boston
2203	9-24-87	1B	Bob Stanley	Boston
2204	9-25-87	1B	Roger Clemens	Boston
2205	9-26-87	1B	Al Nipper	Boston
2206	9-27-87	1B	John Leister	Boston
2207	9-27-87	1B	John Leister	Boston
2208	9-27-87	1B	Bob Stanley	Boston
2209	9-28-87	1B	Mike Flanagan	at Toronto
2210	9-28-87	1B	Mike Flanagan	at Toronto
2211	9-28-87	1B	Mark Eichhorn	at Toronto
2212	9-29-87	1B	Jimmy Key	at Toronto
2213	9-30-87	3B	Dave Stieb	at Toronto
2214	9-30-87	1B	Mark Eichhorn	at Toronto
2215	10-2-87	1B	Jeff Sellers	at Boston
2216	10-3-87	HR-1	John Leister	at Boston
2217	10-3-87	2B	Calvin Schiraldi	at Boston

"I try to play hard every day and play as many games as I can. That's all I can do."

— Robin Yount, 1987

Franklin
Rawlings

ROBIN
1988

HIT	DATE	TYPE	PITCHER	OPPONENT
2218	4-04-88	1B	Mike Boddicker	at Baltimore
2219	4-06-88	1B	Mike Morgan	at Baltimore
2220	4-08-88	HR-1	Lee Guetterman	at New York
2221	4-10-88	HR-1	Tommy John	at New York
2222	4-10-88	1B	Tommy John	at New York
2223	4-10-88	1B	Tim Stoddard	at New York
2224	4-13-88	1B	Dennis Boyd	at Boston
2225	4-15-88	1B	Cecilio Guante	New York
2226	4-16-88	2B	Rick Rhoden	New York
2227	4-16-88	HR-2	Rick Rhoden	New York
2228	4-17-88	HR-2	John Candelaria	New York
2229	4-19-88	1B	Dave Schmidt	Baltimore
2230	4-20-88	1B	Mike Boddicker	Baltimore
2231	4-20-88	HR-1	Mike Boddicker	Baltimore
2232	4-20-88	1B	Tom Neidenfuer	Baltimore
2233	4-21-88	1B	Scott McGregor	Baltimore
2234	4-25-88	1B	Bruce Hurst	Boston
2235	4-27-88	2B	Paul Kilgus	at Texas
2236	4-29-88	2B	Bret Saberhagen	Kansas City
2237	4-30-88	1B	Steve Farr	Kansas City
2238	5-02-88	3B	Bert Blyleven	Minnesota
2239	5-03-88	1B	Allan Anderson	Minnesota
2240	5-06-88	1B	Floyd Bannister	at Kansas City
2241	5-07-88	1B	Bret Saberhagen	at Kansas City
2242	5-07-88	1B	Bret Saberhagen	at Kansas City
2243	5-07-88	2B	Bret Saberhagen	at Kansas City
2244	5-08-88	1B	Gene Garber	at Kansas City
2245	5-09-88	2B	Charlie Lea	at Minnesota
2246	5-09-88	1B	Juan Berenguer	at Minnesota
2247	5-09-88	1B	Karl Best	at Minnesota
2248	5-10-88	1B	Frank Viola	at Minnesota
2249	5-12-88	1B	Tom Candiotti	Cleveland
2250	5-13-88	2B	Greg Swindell	Cleveland
2251	5-13-88	1B	Greg Swindell	Cleveland
2252	5-14-88	1B	John Farrell	Cleveland
2253	5-15-88	HR-1	Scott Bailes	Cleveland
2254	5-15-88	1B	Chris Codiroli	Cleveland
2255	5-16-88	2B	Walt Terrell	Detroit
2256	5-17-88	1B	Paul Gibson	Detroit
2257	5-18-88	1B	Doyle Alexander	Detroit
2258	5-18-88	1B	Doyle Alexander	Detroit
2259	5-20-88	1B	Jim Clancy	Toronto
2260	5-21-88	1B	Dave Stieb	Toronto
2261	5-21-88	1B	Dave Stieb	Toronto
2262	5-21-88	1B	Tom Henke	Toronto
2263	5-22-88	HR-2	Jose Nunez	Toronto
2264	5-22-88	1B	Jose Nunez	Toronto
2265	5-23-88	1B	Todd Stottlemyre	Toronto
2266	5-24-88	2B	Paul Gibson	at Detroit
2267	5-24-88	1B	Paul Gibson	at Detroit
2268	5-26-88	1B	Frank Tanana	at Detroit
2269	5-29-88	1B	Tom Candiotti	at Cleveland
2270	5-30-88	1B	Jim Clancy	at Toronto
2271	6-01-88	1B	Mike Flanagan	at Toronto
2272	6-01-88	1B	Mike Flanagan	at Toronto
2273	6-03-88	2B	Mike Witt	California
2274	6-03-88	2B	Mike Witt	California
2275	6-05-88	3B	Bryan Harvey	California
2276	6-07-88	3B	Bill Swift	at Seattle
2277	6-08-88	2B	Mike Campbell	at Seattle
2278	6-08-88	1B	Mike Campbell	at Seattle
2279	6-08-88	2B	Mike Jackson	at Seattle
2280	6-10-88	3B	Jack McDowell	at Chicago
2281	6-10-88	1B	Jack McDowell	at Chicago
2282	6-12-88	1B	Joel Davis	at Chicago
2283	6-12-88	HR-2	Joel Davis	at Chicago
2284	6-12-88	2B	Bill Long	at Chicago
2285	6-12-88	3B	Steve Rosenberg	at Chicago
2286	6-13-88	2B	Mike Campbell	Seattle
2287	6-14-88	1B	Mike Moore	Seattle
2288	6-15-88	1B	Mark Langston	Seattle
2289	6-16-88	1B	Jerry Reuss	Chicago
2290	6-16-88	1B	Jerry Reuss	Chicago
2291	6-17-88	1B	Bill Long	Chicago
2292	6-17-88	1B	Bill Long	Chicago
2293	6-18-88	3B	Melido Perez	Chicago
2294	6-18-88	1B	Joel Davis	Chicago
2295	6-19-88	1B	Dave LaPoint	Chicago
2296	6-21-88	1B	Curt Young	Oakland
2297	6-21-88	1B	Eric Plunk	Oakland
2298	6-25-88	2B	Mike Witt	at California
2299	6-25-88	1B	Mike Witt	at California
2300	6-26-88	1B	Wille Fraser	at California
2301	6-27-88	1B	Todd Burns	at Oakland
2302	6-28-88	2B	Storm Davis	at Oakland
2303	6-28-88	3B	Storm Davis	at Oakland
2304	6-29-88	1B	Bob Welch	at Oakland
2305	7-01-88	1B	Frank Viola	Minnesota
2306	7-02-88	1B	Charlie Lea	Minnesota
2307	7-02-88	1B	Charlie Lea	Minnesota
2308	7-02-88	1B	Charlie Lea	Minnesota
2309	7-03-88	1B	Keith Atherton	Minnesota
2310	7-04-88	1B	Allan Anderson	Minnesota
2311	7-06-88	2B	Bret Saberhagen	at Kansas City
2312	7-06-88	2B	Bret Saberhagen	at Kansas City
2313	7-06-88	3B	Bret Saberhagen	at Kansas City
2314	7-07-88	1B	Charlie Leibrandt	at Kansas City
2315	7-08-88	1B	Bert Blyleven	at Minnesota
2316	7-08-88	2B	Bert Blyleven	at Minnesota
2317	7-10-88	1B	Fred Toliver	at Minnesota
2318	7-10-88	1B	Juan Berenguer	at Minnesota
2319	7-14-88	1B	Charlie Hough	at Texas
2320	7-14-88	2B	Charlie Hough	at Texas
2321	7-14-88	1B	Ed Vande Berg	at Texas
2322	7-16-88	HR-1	Jeff Russell	at Texas
2323	7-16-88	1B	Jeff Russell	at Texas
2324	7-16-88	1B	Ed Vande Berg	at Texas
2325	7-17-88	2B	Bobby Witt	at Texas
2326	7-17-88	1B	Bobby Witt	at Texas
2327	7-19-88	1B	Bret Saberhagen	Kansas City
2328	7-19-88	1B	Bret Saberhagen	Kansas City
2329	7-21-88	1B	Jose Guzman	Texas
2330	7-21-88	3B	Jose Guzman	Texas
2331	7-22-88	1B	Jeff Russell	Texas
2332	7-23-88	2B	Bobby Witt	Texas
2333	7-26-88	1B	Rick Rhoden	at New York
2334	7-27-88	1B	Tommy John	at New York
2335	7-28-88	1B	Tim Stoddard	at New York
2336	7-28-88	1B	Tim Stoddard	at New York
2337	7-29-88	2B	Dennis Lamp	at Boston(2)
2338	7-31-88	1B	Mike Boddicker	at Boston
2339	8-02-88	1B	Tommy John	New York
2340	8-02-88	1B	Tim Stoddard	New York
2341	8-03-88	2B	Dave Righetti	New York
2342	8-05-88	1B	Jose Bautista	at Baltimore(1)
2343	8-05-88	1B	Mike Morgan	at Baltimore(2)
2344	8-05-88	1B	Mike Morgan	at Baltimore(2)
2345	8-07-88	2B	Jeff Ballard	at Baltimore
2346	8-07-88	2B	Jeff Ballard	at Baltimore
2347	8-09-88	1B	Roger Clemens	Boston(1)
2348	8-09-88	1B	Bob Stanley	Boston(2)
2349	8-11-88	1B	Wes Gardner	Boston
2350	8-12-88	2B	Oswaldo Peraza	Baltimore
2351	8-12-88	1B	Mark Thurmond	Baltimore
2352	8-13-88	1B	Jeff Ballard	Baltimore
2353	8-15-88	1B	Jose Bautista	Baltimore
2354	8-16-88	1B	Rod Nichols	at Cleveland
2355	8-16-88	1B	Rod Nichols	at Cleveland
2356	8-17-88	1B	John Farrell	at Cleveland
2357	8-18-88	3B	Rich Yett	at Cleveland
2358	8-18-88	1B	Rich Yett	at Cleveland
2359	8-19-88	1B	Duane Ward	at Toronto
2360	8-19-88	2B	Duane Ward	at Toronto
2361	8-20-88	1B	Mike Flanagan	at Toronto
2362	8-20-88	HR-1	Mike Flanagan	at Toronto
2363	8-21-88	1B	Jimmy Key	at Toronto
2364	8-21-88	1B	Jimmy Key	at Toronto
2365	8-22-88	1B	John Farrell	Cleveland
2366	8-23-88	1B	Don Gordon	Cleveland
2367	8-24-88	1B	Tom Candiotti	Cleveland
2368	8-25-88	1B	Richard Dotson	New York
2369	8-27-88	1B	Jack Morris	Detroit
2370	8-27-88	1B	Jack Morris	Detroit
2371	8-27-88	1B	Mike Henneman	Detroit
2372	8-30-88	1B	Jeff Musselman	Toronto
2373	8-30-88	1B	Duane Ward	Toronto
2374	8-31-88	1B	Mike Flanagan	Toronto
2375	8-31-88	HR-1	Mike Flanagan	Toronto
2376	9-01-88	1B	Doyle Alexander	at Detroit
2377	9-02-88	1B	Frank Tanana	at Detroit
2378	9-02-88	2B	Don Heinkel	at Detroit
2379	9-03-88	1B	Ted Power	at Detroit
2380	9-04-88	2B	Walt Terrell	at Detroit
2381	9-05-88	2B	Shawn Hillegas	Chicago
2382	9-07-88	1B	Jerry Reuss	Chicago
2383	9-11-88	1B	Mike Campbell	Seattle
2384	9-11-88	2B	Mike Campbell	Seattle
2385	9-12-88	1B	Jerry Reuss	at Chicago
2386	9-12-88	1B	Jerry Reuss	at Chicago
2387	9-13-88	HR-1	Ken Patterson	at Chicago
2388	9-13-88	2B	Ken Patterson	at Chicago
2389	9-13-88	1B	Donn Pall	at Chicago
2390	9-14-88	1B	Bill Long	at Chicago
2391	9-14-88	3B	Bill Long	at Chicago
2392	9-16-88	2B	Erik Hanson	at Seattle
2393	9-18-88	1B	Jerry Reed	at Seattle
2394	9-19-88	1B	Mike Witt	at California
2395	9-19-88	1B	Mike Witt	at California
2396	9-21-88	2B	Willie Fraser	at California
2397	9-24-88	1B	Dave Stewart	Oakland
2398	9-24-88	1B	Dave Stewart	Oakland
2399	9-24-88	2B	Dave Stewart	Oakland
2400	9-24-88	1B	Dave Stewart	Oakland
2401	9-25-88	1B	Storm Davis	Oakland
2402	9-25-88	HR-1	Storm Davis	Oakland
2403	9-25-88	2B	Storm Davis	Oakland
2404	9-27-88	1B	Rich Monteleone	California
2405	9-28-88	1B	Chuck Finley	California
2406	10-1-88	1B	Storm Davis	at Oakland
2407	10-2-88	2B	Bob Welch	at Oakland

"Everybody's got something they can do in life, and it just happened that I could play some baseball." *— Robin Yount, 1988*

BREWERS
19

MVP
1989

HIT	DATE	TYPE	PITCHER	OPPONENT
2408	4-06-89	2B	Bud Black	at Cleveland
2409	4-06-89	3B	Bud Black	at Cleveland
2410	4-08-89	1B	Frank Tanana	at Detroit
2411	4-10-89	2B	Brad Arnsberg	Texas
2412	4-12-89	1B	Craig McMurtry	Texas
2413	4-13-89	1B	Bobby Witt	Texas
2414	4-13-89	1B	Bobby Witt	Texas
2415	4-13-89	1B	Bobby Witt	Texas
2416	4-14-89	1B	Greg Swindell	Cleveland
2417	4-14-89	3B	Joe Skalski	Cleveland
2418	4-15-89	1B	Tom Candiotti	Cleveland
2419	4-16-89	1B	John Farrell	Cleveland
2420	4-16-89	2B	Keith Atherton	Cleveland
2421	4-17-89	1B	Nolan Ryan	at Texas
2422	4-17-89	1B	Brad Arnsberg	at Texas
2423	4-22-89	1B	Charles Hudson	Detroit
2424	4-22-89	3B	Charles Hudson	Detroit
2425	4-23-89	1B	Jeff Robinson	Detroit
2426	4-24-89	1B	Frank Viola	Minnesota
2427	4-26-89	1B	Fred Toliver	Minnesota
2428	4-29-89	1B	Bret Saberhagen	at Kansas City
2429	4-30-89	1B	Floyd Bannister	at Kansas City
2430	5-01-89	1B	Jerry Reuss	at Chicago
2431	5-02-89	1B	Eric King	at Chicago
2432	5-03-89	1B	Shane Rawley	at Minnesota
2433	5-03-89	1B	Francisco Oliveros	at Minnesota
2434	5-04-89	1B	Frank Viola	at Minnesota
2435	5-04-89	1B	Frank Viola	at Minnesota
2436	5-05-89	HR-1	Floyd Bannister	Kansas City
2437	5-06-89	1B	Mark Gubicza	Kansas City
2438	5-07-89	2B	Charlie Leibrandt	Kansas City
2439	5-07-89	2b	Charlie Leibrandt	Kansas City
2440	5-07-89	1B	Luis Aquino	Kansas City
2441	5-09-89	1B	Shawn Hillegas	Chicago
2442	5-10-89	HR-2	Melido Perez	Chicago
2443	5-13-89	2B	Bob Welch	at Oakland
2444	5-14-89	1B	Mike Moore	at Oakland
2445	5-15-89	1B	Dave Stewart	at Oakland
2446	5-16-89	3B	Mark Langston	at Seattle
2447	5-16-89	2B	Mike Schooler	at Seattle
2448	5-17-89	1B	Scott Bankhead	at Seattle
2449	5-19-89	1B	Chuck Finley	at California
2450	5-19-89	2B	Chuck Finley	at California
2451	5-20-89	1B	Bert Blyleven	at California
2452	5-21-89	1B	Kirk McCaskill	at California
2453	5-23-89	1B	Greg Cadaret	Oakland
2454	5-25-89	2B	Dave Stewart	Oakland
2455	5-25-89	1B	Dave Stewart	Oakland
2456	5-26-89	HR-1	Luis DeLeon	Seattle
2457	5-26-89	1B	Mike Jackson	Seattle
2458	5-26-89	HR-1	Mike Jackson	Seattle
2459	5-27-89	1B	Scott Bankhead	Seattle
2460	5-27-89	1B	Scott Bankhead	Seattle
2461	5-28-89	1B	Bill Swift	Seattle
2462	5-28-89	2B	Mike Schooler	Seattle
2463	5-29-89	HR-1	Bert Blyleven	California
2464	5-30-89	1B	Greg Minton	California
2465	6-01-89	1B	Dave LaPoint	New York
2466	6-02-89	1B	Dave Righetti	New York
2467	6-04-89	HR-3	Jimmy Jones	New York
2468	6-04-89	1B	Lee Guetterman	New York
2469	6-05-89	1B	Jimmy Key	at Toronto
2470	6-06-89	1B	Duane Ward	at Toronto
2471	6-08-89	1B	Bob Milacki	at Baltimore
2472	6-09-89	1B	Mark Williamson	at Baltimore
2473	6-10-89	1B	Mark Huismann	at Baltimore
2474	6-10-89	2B	Mark Thurmond	at Baltimore
2475	6-11-89	1B	Jay Tibbs	at Baltimore
2476	6-13-89	1B	Frank Wills	Toronto
2477	6-13-89	1B	Duane Ward	Toronto
2478	6-14-89	1B	Dave Stieb	Toronto
2479	6-17-89	1B	Roy Smith	at Minnesota
2480	6-18-89	1B	Frank Viola	at Minnesota
2481	6-18-89	1B	Jeff Reardon	at Minnesota
2482	6-19-89	2B	Steve Shields	at Minnesota
2483	6-19-89	1B	Juan Berenguer	at Minnesota
2484	6-20-89	1B	Tom Gordon	Kansas City
2485	6-22-89	1B	Jeff Montgomery	Kansas City
2486	6-23-89	1B	Tom McCarthy	Chicago(1)
2487	6-23-89	2B	Tom McCarthy	Chicago(1)
2488	6-23-89	HR-3	Tom McCarthy	Chicago(1)
2489	6-23-89	HR-1	Melido Perez	Chicago(2)
2490	6-25-89	2B	Jerry Reuss	Chicago
2491	6-25-89	2B	Jerry Reuss	Chicago
2492	6-27-89	1B	Roger Clemens	Boston
2493	6-28-89	1B	Mike Smithson	Boston
2494	6-29-89	1B	John Dopson	Boston
2495	6-29-89	2B	John Dopson	Boston
2496	6-30-89	1B	Andy Hawkins	at New York
2497	6-30-89	1B	Andy Hawkins	at New York
2498	7-01-89	1B	Clay Parker	at New York
2499	7-02-89	HR-1	Lance McCullers	at New York
2500	7-02-89	1B	Jimmy Jones	at New York
2501	7-02-89	1B	Jimmy Jones	at New York
2502	7-03-89	1B	Dave Eiland	at New York
2503	7-07-89	HR-1	Pete Harnisch	Baltimore
2504	7-08-89	1B	Brian Holton	Baltimore
2505	7-08-89	2B	Mark Williamson	Baltimore
2506	7-09-89	2B	Dave Schmidt	Baltimore
2507	7-13-89	1B	Jerry Reuss	at Chicago
2508	7-14-89	1B	Greg Hibbard	at Chicago
2509	7-14-89	3B	Bill Long	at Chicago
2510	7-15-89	2B	Melido Perez	at Chicago
2511	7-15-89	2B	Melido Perez	at Chicago
2512	7-15-89	1B	Shawn Hillegas	at Chicago
2513	7-16-89	1B	Richard Dotson	at Chicago
2514	7-17-89	1B	Tom Gordon	at Kansas City
2515	7-17-89	1B	Tom Gordon	at Kansas City
2516	7-18-89	1B	Mark Gubicza	at Kansas City
2517	7-18-89	1B	Mark Gubicza	at Kansas City
2518	7-19-89	2B	Charlie Leibrandt	at Kansas City
2519	7-19-89	1B	Charlie Leibrandt	at Kansas City
2520	7-21-89	1B	Shane Rawley	Minnesota
2521	7-21-89	1B	Shane Rawley	Minnesota
2522	7-22-89	1B	Roy Smith	Minnesota
2523	7-23-89	HR-1	Frank Viola	Minnesota
2524	7-23-89	2B	Frank Viola	Minnesota
2525	7-24-89	1B	Jack Morris	Detroit
2526	7-25-89	1B	Doyle Alexander	Detroit
2527	7-25-89	1B	Doyle Alexander	Detroit
2528	7-26-89	HR-2	Frank Tanana	Detroit
2529	7-27-89	1B	Charles Hudson	Detroit
2530	7-27-89	1B	Charles Hudson	Detroit
2531	7-28-89	2B	Mike Jeffcoat	at Texas
2532	7-28-89	2B	Kenny Rogers	at Texas
2533	7-29-89	2B	Bobby Witt	at Texas
2534	7-29-89	3B	Drew Hall	at Texas
2535	7-29-89	2B	Drew Hall	at Texas
2536	7-31-89	HR-1	Scott Bailes	Cleveland
2537	7-31-89	2B	Steve Olin	Cleveland
2538	8-01-89	2B	Doug Jones	Cleveland
2539	8-02-89	1B	Tom Candiotti	Cleveland
2540	8-04-89	1B	Willie Fraser	California
2541	8-05-89	1B	Mike Witt	California
2542	8-07-89	1B	Kevin Ritz	at Detroit(1)
2543	8-07-89	2B	Paul Gibson	at Detroit(2)
2544	8-08-89	HR-1	Jeff Robinson	at Detroit
2545	8-09-89	1B	Jack Morris	at Detroit
2546	8-09-89	1B	Jack Morris	at Detroit
2547	8-10-89	1B	Bud Black	at Cleveland
2548	8-10-89	2B	Rich Yett	at Cleveland
2549	8-10-89	1B	Rich Yett	at Cleveland
2550	8-10-89	1B	Kevin Wickander	at Cleveland
2551	8-11-89	1B	John Farrell	at Cleveland(1)
2552	8-12-89	1B	Scott Bailes	at Cleveland
2553	8-12-89	3B	Scott Bailes	at Cleveland
2554	8-12-89	1B	Rich Yett	at Cleveland
2555	8-13-89	1B	Tom Candiotti	at Cleveland
2556	8-14-89	2B	Andy Hawkins	New York
2557	8-16-89	2B	Walt Terrell	New York
2558	8-17-89	3B	Wes Gardner	Boston
2559	8-17-89	1B	Rob Murphy	Boston
2560	8-18-89	1B	Bob Stanley	Boston
2561	8-19-89	1B	Mike Boddicker	Boston
2562	8-20-89	1B	Mike Smithson	Boston
2563	8-21-89	1B	Jeff Ballard	at Baltimore
2564	8-26-89	1B	Dave Stieb	at Toronto
2565	8-27-89	2B	Todd Stottlemyre	at Toronto
2566	8-28-89	HR-1	John Cerutti	at Toronto
2567	8-28-89	1B	John Cerutti	at Toronto
2568	8-28-89	1B	Mauro Gozzo	at Toronto
2569	8-29-89	HR-3	Eric Hanson	Seattle
2570	8-31-89	1B	Brian Holman	Seattle
2571	8-31-89	3B	Brian Holman	Seattle
2572	9-01-89	1B	Bob Welch	Oakland
2573	9-01-89	1B	Todd Burns	Oakland
2574	9-02-89	2B	Dave Stewart	Oakland
2575	9-05-89	HR-1	Kirk McCaskill	at California
2576	9-06-89	HR-2	Dan Petry	at California
2577	9-06-89	1B	Rich Monteleone	at California
2578	9-07-89	1B	Mike Witt	at California
2579	9-09-89	1B	Mike Jackson	at Seattle
2580	9-09-89	1B	Jerry Reed	at Seattle
2581	9-10-89	2B	Randy Johnson	at Seattle
2582	9-10-89	2B	Randy Johnson	at Seattle
2583	9-10-89	1B	Bill Swift	at Seattle
2584	9-12-89	1B	Matt Young	at Oakland
2585	9-13-89	2B	Dave Stewart	at Oakland
2586	9-17-89	1B	Bobby Witt	Texas
2587	9-17-89	1B	Bobby Witt	Texas
2588	9-21-89	1B	Greg Cadaret	at New York(1)
2589	9-21-89	1B	Greg Cadaret	at New York(1)
2590	9-21-89	1B	Kevin Mmahat	at New York(1)
2591	9-21-89	1B	Andy Hawkins	at New York(2)
2592	9-21-89	1B	Andy Hawkins	at New York(2)
2593	9-22-89	1B	Jim Acker	Toronto
2594	9-24-89	HR-1	John Cerutti	Toronto
2595	9-24-89	1B	John Cerutti	Toronto
2596	9-28-89	HR-2	Mike Boddicker	at Boston
2597	9-28-89	1B	Mike Smithson	at Boston
2598	9-28-89	1B	Rob Murphy	at Boston
2599	9-29-89	1B	Dennis Boyd	at Boston
2600	9-30-89	2B	Roger Clemens	at Boston
2601	9-30-89	1B	Roger Clemens	at Boston
2602	10-1-89	HR-1	John Dopson	at Boston

"I believe if you concentrate on playing the game as hard as you can, the numbers will take care of themselves." — *Robin Yount, 1989*

Brewers
19
PONY

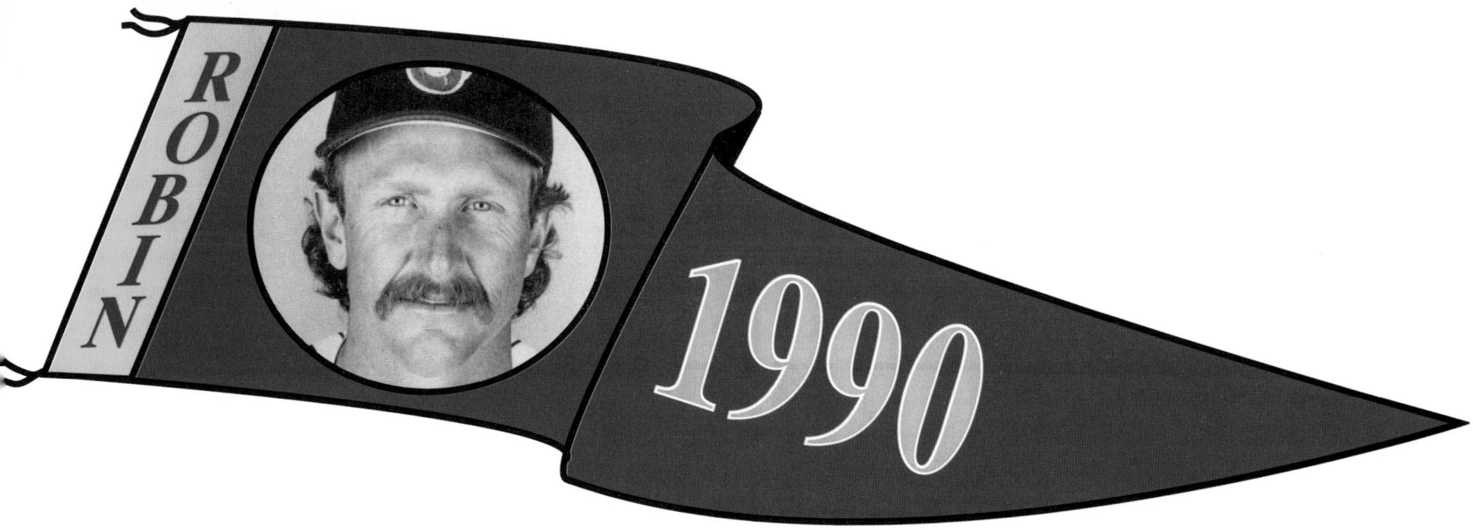
ROBIN
1990

HIT	DATE	TYPE	PITCHER	OPPONENT
2603	4-10-90	1B	Eric King	Chicago
2604	4-13-90	1B	John Leister	at Boston
2605	4-14-90	1B	Roger Clemens	at Boston
2606	4-14-90	1B	Roger Clemens	at Boston
2607	4-16-90	1B	Mike Rochford	at Boston
2608	4-17-90	1B	Kevin Brown	at Texas
2609	4-18-90	1B	Jamie Moyer	at Texas
2610	4-18-90	1B	Gary Mielke	at Texas
2611	4-19-90	1B	Bobby Witt	at Texas
2612	4-19-90	3B	Bobby Witt	at Texas
2613	4-22-90	1B	Lee Smith	Boston
2614	4-24-90	2B	Richard Dotson	Kansas City
2615	4-26-90	1B	Mark Gubicza	Kansas City
2616	4-27-90	2B	Jack Morris	at Detroit
2617	4-27-90	1B	Jack Morris	at Detroit
2618	4-28-90	HR-3	Frank Tanana	at Detroit
2619	4-28-90	1B	Frank Tanana	at Detroit
2620	4-30-90	HR-1	Jeff Robinson	at Detroit
2621	4-30-90	1B	Jeff Robinson	at Detroit
2622	5-01-90	1B	Bret Saberhagen	at Kansas City
2623	5-01-90	1B	Bret Saberhagen	at Kansas City
2624	5-03-90	HR-3	Mark Gubicza	at Kansas City
2625	5-05-90	2B	Roy Smith	Minnesota
2626	5-08-90	1B	Frank Tanana	Detroit
2627	5-09-90	1B	Dan Petry	Detroit
2628	5-09-90	1B	Mike Henneman	Detroit
2629	5-13-90	1B	David West	at Minnesota
2630	5-13-90	1B	Juan Berenguer	at Minnesota
2631	5-15-90	1B	Mark Langston	California
2632	5-15-90	3B	Mark Langston	California
2633	5-15-90	1B	Mark Eichhorn	California
2634	5-16-90	1B	Jim Abbott	California
2635	5-17-90	1B	Willie Fraser	California
2636	5-19-90	1B	Dave Stewart	Oakland
2637	5-23-90	1B	Mike Moore	Oakland
2638	5-24-90	1B	Dave Stewart	at Oakland
2639	5-25-90	1B	Mark Langston	at California
2640	5-25-90	1B	Mark Langston	at California
2641	5-26-90	1B	Bert Blyleven	at California
2642	5-27-90	1B	Chuck Finley	at California
2643	5-29-90	1B	Mike Jackson	at Seattle
2644	5-30-90	1B	Bryan Clark	at Seattle
2645	6-02-90	1B	John Cerutti	at Toronto
2646	6-05-90	1B	Brian Holton	Baltimore
2647	6-06-90	HR-2	Jeff Ballard	Baltimore
2648	6-06-90	2B	Jeff Ballard	Baltimore
2649	6-06-90	1B	Mark Williamson	Baltimore
2650	6-07-90	1B	Dave Johnson	Baltimore
2651	6-07-90	1B	Dave Johnson	Baltimore
2652	6-08-90	1B	Tom Henke	Toronto
2653	6-12-90	1B	Mark Williamson	at Baltimore
2654	6-13-90	1B	Dave Johnson	at Baltimore
2655	6-13-90	1B	Juan Bautista	at Baltimore
2656	6-15-90	1B	Tom Candiotti	at Cleveland
2657	6-16-90	1B	Cecilio Guante	at Cleveland
2658	6-17-90	HR-1	Bud Black	at Cleveland
2659	6-18-90	1B	Tim Leary	New York
2660	6-20-90	1B	Alan Mills	New York
2661	6-22-90	2B	Cecilio Guante	Cleveland
2662	6-23-90	1B	Jeff Kaiser	Cleveland
2663	6-23-90	1B	Rudy Seanez	Cleveland
2664	6-24-90	1B	John Farrell	Cleveland
2665	6-24-90	1B	Sergio Valdez	Cleveland
2666	6-24-90	HR-1	Sergio Valdez	Cleveland
2667	6-28-90	1B	Tim Leary	at New York
2668	6-29-90	1B	Randy Johnson	at Seattle
2669	6-30-90	1B	Erik Hanson	at Seattle
2670	6-30-90	HR-2	Erik Hanson	at Seattle
2671	7-01-90	1B	Brian Holman	at Seattle
2672	7-03-90	1B	Curt Young	Oakland
2673	7-04-90	3B	Mike Norris	Oakland
2674	7-08-90	1B	Mark Eichhorn	California
2675	7-11-90	1B	Jack McDowell	at Chicago
2676	7-11-90	HR-3	Jack McDowell	at Chicago
2677	7-13-90	1B	Dave Stewart	at Oakland
2678	7-13-90	2B	Todd Burns	at Oakland
2679	7-16-90	1B	Mark Langston	at California
2680	7-16-90	1B	Mark Langston	at California
2681	7-17-90	1B	Kirk McCaskill	at California
2682	7-18-90	1B	Jim Abbott	at California
2683	7-18-90	1B	Jim Abbott	at California
2684	7-20-90	1B	Bill Swift	Seattle
2685	7-20-90	1B	Bill Swift	Seattle
2686	7-20-90	2B	Bill Swift	Seattle
2687	7-21-90	1B	Erik Hanson	Seattle
2688	7-22-90	HR-2	Brian Holman	Seattle
2689	7-23-90	HR-1	Mike Boddicker	Boston
2690	7-23-90	2B	Dennis Lamp	Boston
2691	7-24-90	3B	Greg Harris	Boston
2692	7-27-90	1B	Jack McDowell	at Chicago
2693	7-27-90	1B	Bobby Thigpen	at Chicago
2694	7-29-90	1B	Greg Hibbard	at Chicago
2695	7-31-90	3B	Nolan Ryan	Texas
2696	8-02-90	1B	Alex Fernandez	Chicago
2697	8-03-90	1B	Greg Hibbard	Chicago
2698	8-03-90	HR-1	Greg Hibbard	Chicago
2699	8-06-90	2B	Roy Smith	at Minnesota
2700	8-06-90	1B	Roy Smith	at Minnesota
2701	8-07-90	2B	Mark Guthrie	at Minnesota
2702	8-10-90	1B	Andy McGaffigan	at K.C.(1)
2703	8-10-90	1B	Jeff Montgomery	at K.C.(1)
2704	8-11-90	1B	Pete Filson	at Kansas City
2705	8-11-90	1B	Steve Farr	at Kansas City
2706	8-15-90	1B	Steve Searcy	at Detroit
2707	8-15-90	1B	Steve Searcy	at Detroit
2708	8-16-90	HR-1	Dan Petry	at Detroit
2709	8-18-90	1B	Steve Crawford	Kansas City
2710	8-22-90	HR-2	Tom Candiotti	Cleveland
2711	8-27-90	1B	Frank Wills	at Toronto
2712	8-27-90	1B	Jim Acker	at Toronto
2713	8-28-90	1B	Dave Stieb	at Toronto
2714	8-31-90	1B	John Mitchell	Baltimore
2715	9-01-90	1B	Ben McDonald	Baltimore
2716	9-03-90	1B	Mark Guthrie	Minnesota(1)
2717	9-04-90	1B	Tim Drummond	Minnesota
2718	9-05-90	1B	Juan Berenguer	Minnesota
2719	9-07-90	HR-3	Jack Morris	Detroit
2720	9-08-90	2B	Paul Gibson	Detroit
2721	9-09-90	2B	Scott Aldred	Detroit
2722	9-10-90	2B	Greg Harris	at Boston(1)
2723	9-10-90	1B	Greg Harris	at Boston(1)
2724	9-10-90	1B	Jeff Gray	at Boston(1)
2725	9-10-90	1B	Dana Kiecker	at Boston(2)
2726	9-10-90	1B	Dana Kiecker	at Boston(2)
2727	9-11-90	HR-2	Wes Gardner	at Boston
2728	9-12-90	1B	Mike Boddicker	at Boston
2729	9-14-90	HR-1	Nolan Ryan	at Texas
2730	9-14-90	1B	Kenny Rogers	at Texas
2731	9-15-90	2B	Gerald Alexander	at Texas
2732	9-15-90	1B	Gerald Alexander	at Texas
2733	9-15-90	1B	Jamie Moyer	at Texas
2734	9-16-90	1B	Scott Chiamparino	at Texas
2735	9-17-90	1B	Steve Olin	at Cleveland
2736	9-18-90	1B	Charles Nagy	at Cleveland
2737	9-24-90	1B	John Candelaria	Toronto
2738	9-25-90	HR-2	Bud Black	Toronto
2739	9-25-90	2B	Bud Black	Toronto
2740	9-25-90	1B	Duane Ward	Toronto
2741	9-26-90	1B	David Wells	Toronto
2742	9-26-90	1B	Jim Acker	Toronto
2743	9-30-90	1B	Dave Eiland	New York
2744	10-1-90	2B	Jeff Russell	New York
2745	10-2-90	1B	Kenny Rogers	Texas
2746	10-2-90	1B	Kenny Rogers	Texas
2747	10-3-90	1B	Brad Arnsberg	Texas

"I'm grateful for all the Milwaukee and Wisconsin fans support . . . I'm looking forward to being with the Brewers." *— Robin Yount, 1990*

19

YOUNT
1991

HIT	DATE	TYPE	PITCHER	OPPONENT
2748	4-08-91	HR-2	Nolan Ryan	at Texas
2749	4-08-91	1B	Nolan Ryan	at Texas
2750	4-10-91	1B	Kevin Brown	at Texas
2751	4-10-91	1B	John Barfield	at Texas
2752	4-11-91	1B	David Wells	at Toronto
2753	4-12-91	1B	Dennis Boucher	at Toronto
2754	4-13-91	1B	Frank Wills	at Toronto
2755	4-14-91	1B	Jimmy Key	at Toronto
2756	4-18-91	2B	Jeff Ballard	Baltimore
2757	4-18-91	2B	Jeff Ballard	Baltimore
2758	4-18-91	HR-1	Jose Bautista	Baltimore
2759	4-19-91	3B	Dave Stieb	Toronto
2760	4-19-91	1B	Dave Stieb	Toronto
2761	4-20-91	1B	Jimmy Key	Toronto
2762	4-21-91	HR-3	Frank Wills	Toronto
2763	4-23-91	2B	Bobby Witt	Texas
2764	4-23-91	HR-3	Bobby Witt	Texas
2765	4-23-91	1B	Gerald Alexander	Texas
2766	4-25-91	HR-2	John Barfield	Texas
2767	4-26-91	2B	Jose Mesa	at Baltimore
2768	4-26-91	1B	Paul Kilgus	at Baltimore
2769	4-27-91	2B	Mark Williamson	at Baltimore
2770	4-27-91	1B	Gregg Olson	at Baltimore
2771	4-28-91	1B	Ben McDonald	at Baltimore
2772	4-28-91	1B	Ben McDonald	at Baltimore
2773	4-30-91	1B	Alex Fernandez	Chicago
2774	5-02-91	1B	Kevin Tapani	Minnesota
2775	5-04-91	1B	Mark Guthrie	Minnesota
2776	5-07-91	1B	Greg Hibbard	at Chicago
2777	5-10-91	2B	Bret Saberhagen	Kansas City
2778	5-11-91	HR-2	Tom Gordon	Kansas City
2779	5-12-91	1B	Mike Boddicker	Kansas City
2780	5-12-91	HR-1	Mike Boddicker	Kansas City
2781	5-15-91	2B	Kevin Tapani	at Minnesota
2782	5-16-91	HR-1	Allan Anderson	at Minnesota
2783	5-16-91	1B	Allan Anderson	at Minnesota
2784	5-17-91	2B	Tom Gordon	at Kansas City
2785	5-17-91	1B	Mark Davis	at Kansas City
2786	5-18-91	1B	Storm Davis	at Kansas City
2787	5-18-91	1B	Kevin Appier	at Kansas City
2788	5-19-91	1B	Mark Gubicza	at Kansas City
2789	5-19-91	1B	Luis Aquino	at Kansas City
2790	5-21-91	1B	Joe Hesketh	at Boston
2791	5-22-91	1B	Danny Darwin	at Boston
2792	5-23-91	1B	Charles Nagy	Cleveland
2793	5-24-91	1B	Rod Nichols	Cleveland
2794	5-25-91	1B	Eric King	Cleveland
2795	5-25-91	1B	Eric King	Cleveland
2796	5-26-91	HR-1	Shawn Hillegas	Cleveland
2797	5-27-91	1B	Bill Gullickson	Detroit
2798	5-27-91	1B	Steve Searcy	Detroit
2799	5-28-91	2B	Frank Tanana	Detroit
2800	5-28-91	1B	Dan Petry	Detroit
2801	6-02-91	1B	Wade Taylor	at New York
2802	6-04-91	1B	Dave Stewart	at Oakland
2803	6-08-91	2B	Rich DeLucia	at Seattle
2804	6-10-91	1B	Kirk McCaskill	at California
2805	6-10-91	1B	Scott Bailes	at California
2806	6-11-91	1B	Mark Langston	at California
2807	6-11-91	1B	Mark Langston	at California
2808	6-12-91	2B	F. Valenzuela	at California
2809	6-12-91	1B	Joe Grahe	at California
2810	6-12-91	1B	Joe Grahe	at California
2811	6-12-91	1B	Mark Eichhorn	at California
2812	6-15-91	1B	Dave Stewart	Oakland(1)
2813	6-15-91	3B	Andy Hawkins	Oakland(2)
2814	6-17-91	1B	Mike Moore	Oakland
2815	6-18-91	1B	Mike Fetters	California
2816	6-19-91	1B	Mark Eichhorn	California
2817	6-25-91	1B	Walt Terrell	at Detroit
2818	6-29-91	1B	Jeff Johnson	New York
2819	6-29-91	2B	John Habyan	New York
2820	6-30-91	1B	Steve Howe	New York
2821	7-02-91	2B	Tom Bolton	Boston
2822	7-03-91	1B	Greg Harris	Boston
2823	7-03-91	3B	Greg Harris	Boston
2824	7-04-91	1B	Charles Nagy	at Cleveland
2825	7-04-91	1B	Charles Nagy	at Cleveland
2826	7-05-91	1B	Rod Nichols	at Cleveland
2827	8-01-91	1B	Mike Boddicker	Kansas City
2828	8-01-91	1B	Mike Boddicker	Kansas City
2829	8-01-91	1B	Mike Boddicker	Kansas City
2830	8-03-91	1B	Jose Guzman	Texas
2831	8-03-91	1B	Jose Guzman	Texas
2832	8-05-91	2B	Stacy Jones	at Baltimore
2833	8-05-91	1B	Todd Frohwirth	at Baltimore
2834	8-05-91	2B	Mark Williamson	at Baltimore
2835	8-06-91	1B	Mike Flanagan	at Baltimore
2836	8-07-91	1B	Ben McDonald	at Baltimore
2837	8-09-91	1B	Jose Guzman	at Texas
2838	8-09-91	3B	Gerald Alexander	at Texas
2839	8-11-91	1B	Kevin Brown	at Texas
2840	8-11-91	1B	Kevin Brown	at Texas
2841	8-11-91	1B	Mike Jeffcoat	at Texas
2842	8-13-91	1B	Tom Candiotti	Toronto
2843	8-15-91	1B	Todd Stottlemyre	Toronto
2844	8-17-91	1B	Ben McDonald	Baltimore
2845	8-22-91	1B	Juan Guzman	at Toronto
2846	8-22-91	1B	Duane Ward	at Toronto
2847	8-23-91	2B	Dave Stewart	at Oakland
2848	8-23-91	1B	Curt Young	at Oakland
2849	8-23-91	1B	Joe Klink	at Oakland
2850	8-24-91	1B	Joe Slusarski	at Oakland
2851	8-25-91	1B	Ron Darling	at Oakland
2852	8-25-91	1B	Ron Darling	at Oakland
2853	8-26-91	1B	Bill Krueger	at Seattle
2854	8-27-91	2B	Rich DeLucia	at Seattle
2855	8-27-91	1B	Calvin Jones	at Seattle
2856	8-28-91	1B	Russ Swan	at Seattle
2857	8-30-91	1B	Kirk McCaskill	California
2858	8-31-91	2B	Joe Grahe	California
2859	8-31-91	2B	Mark Eichhorn	California
2860	9-01-91	1B	Chuck Finley	California
2861	9-02-91	1B	Jim Abbott	California
2862	9-03-91	HR-3	Dennis Eckersley	Oakland
2863	9-07-91	1B	Bryan Harvey	at California
2864	9-08-91	1B	Jim Abbott	at California
2865	9-12-91	2B	Mark Leiter	Detroit
2866	9-13-91	1B	Bill Gullickson	Detroit
2867	9-14-91	1B	Scott Aldred	Detroit
2868	9-15-91	1B	Dave Haas	Detroit
2869	9-16-91	1B	Wade Taylor	at New York
2870	9-16-91	1B	Lee Guetterman	at New York
2871	9-20-91	1B	Mark Leiter	at Detroit
2872	9-22-91	1B	Walt Terrell	at Detroit
2873	9-24-91	1B	Eric Plunk	New York
2874	9-26-91	1B	Wade Taylor	New York
2875	9-26-91	1B	Wade Taylor	New York
2876	10-4-91	1B	Mike Gardiner	at Boston
2877	10-5-91	1B	Greg Harris	at Boston
2878	10-6-91	1B	Roger Clemens	at Boston

> ***"I don't play this game to see how many numbers I can put up . . . I enjoy the competition of the game."*** *— Robin Yount, 1991*

3000
1992

HIT	DATE	TYPE	PITCHER	OPPONENT
2879	4-06-92	2B	Scott Erickson	Minnesota
2880	4-06-92	1B	Rick Aguilera	Minnesota
2881	4-10-92	1B	Scott Lewis	at California
2882	4-10-92	1B	Scott Lewis	at California
2883	4-11-92	1B	Don Robinson	at California
2884	4-12-92	2B	Mark Langston	at California
2885	4-12-92	1B	Mark Langston	at California
2886	4-12-92	1B	Mark Eichhorn	at California
2887	4-15-92	1B	Rick Aguilera	at Minnesota
2888	4-17-92	1B	Erik Hanson	Seattle
2889	4-18-92	1B	Russ Swan	Seattle
2890	4-19-92	1B	Dave Fleming	Seattle
2891	4-19-92	2B	Dave Fleming	Seattle
2892	4-26-92	1B	Dennis Cook	at Cleveland(2)
2893	4-30-92	1B	David Wells	Toronto
2894	5-01-92	2B	Jimmy Key	Toronto
2895	5-01-92	HR-1	Jimmy Key	Toronto
2896	5-02-92	2B	Jack Morris	Toronto
2897	5-02-92	1B	Jack Morris	Toronto
2898	5-03-92	1B	Dave Stieb	Toronto
2899	5-05-92	2B	Jack McDowell	at Chicago
2900	5-07-92	1B	Curt Young	at Kansas City
2901	5-07-92	1B	Neal Heaton	at Kansas City
2902	5-08-92	1B	Kevin Brown	at Texas
2903	5-09-92	2B	Nolan Ryan	at Texas
2904	5-12-92	2B	Terry Leach	Chicago
2905	5-15-92	1B	Jose Guzman	Texas
2906	5-15-92	2B	Jeff Robinson	Texas
2907	5-16-92	2B	Nolan Ryan	Texas
2908	5-16-92	1B	Nolan Ryan	Texas
2909	5-17-92	1B	Jeff Russell	Texas
2910	5-18-92	HR-1	Eric King	at Detroit
2911	5-20-92	1B	Bill Gullickson	at Detroit
2912	5-20-92	1B	Bill Gullickson	at Detroit
2913	5-21-92	2B	Scott Aldred	at Detroit
2914	5-23-92	HR-1	Shawn Hillegas	at New York
2915	5-24-92	1B	Scott Sanderson	at New York
2916	5-25-92	1B	John Habyan	at New York
2917	5-25-92	1B	Lee Guetterman	at New York
2918	5-26-92	2B	Dave Steib	at Toronto
2919	5-29-92	1B	Shawn Hillegas	New York
2920	6-01-92	1B	Scott Aldred	Detroit
2921	6-02-92	1B	Mark Leiter	Detroit
2922	6-03-92	1B	Kevin Ritz	Detroit
2923	6-03-92	HR-1	Kurt Knudsen	Detroit
2924	6-05-92	1B	Jim Abbott	California
2925	6-05-92	1B	Scott Bailes	California
2926	6-06-92	2B	Bert Blyleven	California
2927	6-07-92	1B	Mark Langston	California
2928	6-07-92	2B	Chuck Crim	California
2929	6-08-92	1B	Joe Slusarski	Oakland
2930	6-08-92	1B	Joe Slusarski	Oakland
2931	6-08-92	1B	Jeff Parrett	Oakland
2932	6-09-92	1B	Rick Honeycutt	Oakland
2933	6-13-92	1B	Randy Kramer	at Seattle
2934	6-13-92	2B	Jeff Nelson	at Seattle
2935	6-14-92	1B	Dave Fleming	at Seattle
2936	6-14-92	1B	Jeff Nelson	at Seattle
2937	6-14-92	HR-2	Jeff Nelson	at Seattle
2938	6-15-92	1B	Kevin Campbell	at Oakland
2939	6-16-92	2B	Joe Slusarski	at Oakland
2940	6-17-92	2B	Mike Moore	at Oakland
2941	6-17-92	1B	Mike Moore	at Oakland
2942	6-19-92	2B	Scott Scudder	Cleveland
2943	6-19-92	2B	Scott Scudder	Cleveland
2944	6-19-92	1B	Ted Power	Cleveland
2945	6-24-92	1B	Bob Milacki	Baltimore
2946	6-24-92	1B	Alan Mills	Baltimore
2947	6-27-92	1B	Roger Clemens	at Boston
2948	6-28-92	2B	Matt Young	at Boston
2949	6-29-92	1B	Bob Milacki	at Baltimore
2950	6-30-92	1B	Rick Sutcliffe	at Baltimore
2951	7-01-92	2B	Ben McDonald	at Baltimore
2952	7-01-92	1B	Alan Mills	at Baltimore
2953	7-02-92	1B	Kevin Appier	at Kansas City
2954	7-03-92	2B	Rusty Meacham	at Kansas City
2955	7-05-92	1B	Mark Gubicza	at K. C.(1)
2956	7-05-92	2B	Mark Davis	at K. C.(2)
2957	7-06-92	1B	Kevin Brown	at Texas
2958	7-08-92	2B	Jose Guzman	at Texas
2959	7-08-92	1B	Jeff Russell	at Texas
2960	7-10-92	1B	Steve Shifflett	Kansas City
2961	7-11-92	1B	Rick Reed	Kansas City
2962	7-11-92	2B	Neal Heaton	Kansas City
2963	7-16-92	1B	Kirk McCaskill	at Chicago
2964	7-19-92	1B	Greg Hibbard	at Chicago
2965	7-20-92	1B	Edwin Nunez	Texas
2966	7-23-92	1B	Jack McDowell	Chicago
2967	7-26-92	2B	Kirk McCaskill	Chicago
2968	7-26-92	1B	Bobby Thigpen	Chicago
2969	7-30-92	2B	Willie Banks	at Minnesota
2970	8-05-92	1B	Randy Johnson	Seattle
2971	8-06-92	1B	Mark Grant	Seattle
2972	8-08-92	2B	Scott Erickson	Minnesota(1)
2973	8-08-92	1B	Carl Willis	Minnesota(1)
2974	8-14-92	1B	Greg Harris	Boston(2)
2975	8-20-92	2B	David Wells	Toronto
2976	8-20-92	3B	David Wells	Toronto
2977	8-20-92	1B	Bob MacDonald	Toronto
2978	8-21-92	1B	John Doherty	Detroit
2979	8-21-92	1B	John Doherty	Detroit
2980	8-22-92	1B	Frank Tanana	Detroit
2981	8-22-92	1B	Frank Tanana	Detroit
2982	8-22-92	1B	Frank Tanana	Detroit
2983	8-24-92	1B	Bob Wickman	at New York
2984	8-24-92	2B	Russ Springer	at New York
2985	8-25-92	2B	Sammy Militello	at New York
2986	8-27-92	1B	Jack Morris	at New York
2987	8-28-92	2B	Doug Linton	at Toronto
2988	8-29-92	3B	David Cone	at Toronto
2989	8-29-92	1B	Doug Linton	at Toronto
2990	8-31-92	1B	Scott Kamieniecki	New York
2991	9-02-92	3B	Scott Sanderson	New York
2992	9-02-92	HR-2	Scott Sanderson	New York
2993	9-04-92	1B	Bill Gullickson	at Detroit
2994	9-05-92	HR-2	David Haas	at Detroit
2995	9-05-92	1B	Les Lancaster	at Detroit
2996	9-06-92	1B	John Doherty	at Detroit
2997	9-06-92	1B	Mike Henneman	at Detroit
2998	9-07-92	1B	Dennis Cook	Cleveland
2999	9-08-92	1B	Jack Armstrong	Cleveland
3000	9-09-92	1B	Jose Mesa	Cleveland

"I don't think it's the game itself that drives me. It's the competitiveness. I enjoy trying to do what it takes to win. There is something very satisfying about winning. That's kind of always been what keeps me going." *— Robin Yount, 1992*

Pitching In!

A Hit List of Contributors

During the 19 seasons it has taken Robin Yount to collect 3,000 hits, there have been a great number of contributors to the cause. They have come in all shapes and sizes, from a big as a Tom **HOUSE** to as Jeff **LITTLE** as a Nate **SNELL**. They came from near and Steve **FARR**; from Rawley **EAST**wick and David **WEST**; from every stop in the alphabet, from Don **A**ase to Geoff **Z**ahn. Age was never a factor. He hit'em off Kip **YOUNG** and Greg **OL**son. Some were Tim **LEARY** to throw him the high Neal **HEAT**on. They knew the ball would Dave **LEIP**er off his bat a Bill **LONG**, long way. Robin Jim **GOTT** the Karl **BEST** of them. One could search from the Brad **HAVENS** to the Mike Bar**LOW** ends of the earth and not find anyone Kevin **APPIER** than Robin, and Rich **YETT**, although he did not have the great Ted **POWER** of some of those in his class, he still knew Jay **HOWELL** to get the job done. Robin played this game to **WIN** Remmerswaal. It was more important to be the **VICTOR** Cruz than to be a baseball Ron **DARLING**. Many say Robin was Rick **WISE** when he was Matt **YOUNG**. He did all the Jim **WRIGHT** things and was Bill **SWIFT** to learn the game. Many concur that over the years, Robin became the Chuck **CRIM** of the crop. It has been Rich **WORTH**am the Rick **WAIT**s to see this Curt **YOUNG** future Drew **HALL** of Famer Vern **RUHLE** the baseball world and be crowned Eric **KING** of swing for 1992.

More Contributors . . . Did You Know?

- In all, Yount managed at least one hit off of 626 pitchers enroute to 3,000 hits.
- The top 4 contributors, Frank Tanana (39), Mike Flanagan (35), Dave Stieb (32) and Jack Morris (31) are still active.
- Yount managed to hit a father-son combination—Mel (3) and Todd (3) Stottlemyre; and 3 brothers acts—Phil (8) and Joe (3) Niekro; Gaylord (14) and Jim (1) Perry; and Tom (10) and Pat (4) Underwood.
- Collected 57 hits off 6 Hall of Famers—Jim Hunter (12), Rollie Fingers (4), Fergie Jenkins (13), Jim Palmer (21), Gaylord Perry (14) and Tom Seaver (7).
- Former and Present Coaches: Ray Burris (4), Bill Castro (1) and Pat Dobson (10).
- Former Teammates: Len Barker (9), Dan Boitano (1), Mark Bomback (3), Pete Broberg (2), Ray Burris (4), Ernie Camacho (1), Mark Clear (1), Tom Candiotti (12), Bill Castro (1), Reggie Cleveland (9), Jim Colburn (2), Chuck Crim (1), Danny Darwin (11), Ed Farmer (4), Rollie Fingers (4), Moose Haas (2), Fred Holdsworth (2), John Henry Johnson (2), Doug Jones (2), Bill Krueger (5), Pete Ladd (1), Dave LaPoint (2), Jack Lazorko (1), Tim Leary (2), Doc Medich (19), Paul Mitchell (3), Paul Mirabella (3), Tom Murphy (7), Edwin Nunez (3), Jerry Reuss (11), Jim Slaton (4), Lary Sorensen (14), Don Sutton (5), Pete Vuckovich (3) and Rick Waits (4).
- Names Of Presidents: Reggie Cleveland (9), Dave Ford (2), Roric Harrison (1), Darrell Jackson (2), Jesse Jefferson (8), Joe Johnson (4), Mark Grant (1) and Bruce Taylor (1).
- Colors Of The Rainbow: Bud Black (13), Vida Blue (12), Kevin Brown (6), Jeff Gray (1), Pete Redfern (5) and Len Whitehouse (2).
- Behind The Wheel: Richard Dotson (18), Dave Ford (2), Don Hood (3), Charles Hudson (6) and Jimmy Key (12).
- Singing Stars: Michael Jackson (5) and Kenny Rogers (4).
- Body And Soul: Mike Armstrong (1), Scott Bankhead (6), Dave Beard (5), Rollie Fingers (4) and Bill Hands (1).
- Change In The Weather: Storm Davis (19), Dave Frost (2), Rich Gale (7) and Chuck Rainey (7).
- Home Sweet Home: Richard Barnes (1), Drew Hall (2), Tom House (4), Dennis Lamp (5), Dan Stanhouse (2), Steve Stone (12), Duane Ward (7), Len Whitehouse (2) and Wilbur Wood (6).
- Get A Job: Steve Baker (1), John Butcher (6), Dennis Cook (2), Ed Farmer (4), Wes Gardner (3), Jim Hunter (12), Mike Marshall (6), Mike Mason (5), Dyar Miller (4), Bill Singer (4), Sammy Stewart (5), Wade Taylor (4), John Tudor (1) and Stefan Wever (2).
- Pet Peeves: Ray Bare (7), Doug Bird (10), Brian Fisher (2), Goose Gossage (6), Catfish Hunter (12), Moose Haas (2), Andy Hawkins (6), Jim Kaat (4), Mike Parrott (9), Russ Swan (2) and Steve Trout (5).
- Multi-Name Players: Jerry Don Gleaton (3), Roy Lee Jackson (3) and John Henry Johnson (2).
- On A First Name Basis: Yount has picked on more players who go by Mike (240), Dave (165) and Jim (128) than any others.
- Any Day Of The Week: A breakdown of his hits on each day of the week shows that Yount enjoyed hitting on the weekend, but particularly on the Sabbath—Sunday (516), Saturday (493), Friday (453), Wednesday (440), Tuesday (434), Thursday (338) and Monday (326).
- Bleacher Balls: Of Yount's 242 home runs, 3 were grand slams, 26 were 3-run shots, 81 were 2-run homers and 132 were solo shots.

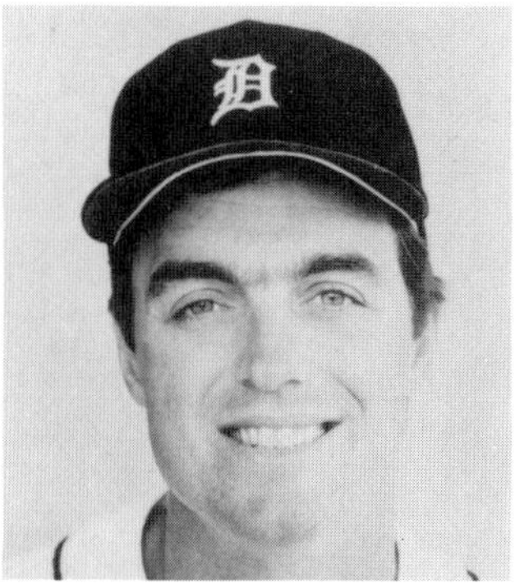

Frank Tanana
39 Hits

	PITCHER	# OF HITS		PITCHER	# OF HITS		PITCHER	# OF HITS
1	Frank Tanana	39	24	Mike Witt	18	47	Bobby Witt	13
2	Mike Flanagan	35	25	Paul Splittorff	18	48	Bud Black	13
3	Dave Steib	32	26	Richard Dotson	18	49	Ferguson Jenkins	13
4	Jack Morris	31	27	Ron Guidry	18	50	Matt Keough	13
5	Mike Torrez	25	28	Bob Stanley	17	51	Milt Wilcox	13
6	Dan Petry	24	29	Mark Gubicza	17	52	Rick Wise	13
7	Doyle Alexander	24	30	Glenn Abbott	16	53	Wayne Garland	13
8	Larry Gura	24	31	Mark Langston	16	54	Andy Hassler	12
9	Tommy John	23	32	Rudy May	16	55	Jim Hunter	12
10	Floyd Bannister	21	33	Scott McGregor	16	56	Jimmy Key	12
11	Jim Clancy	21	34	Charlie Hough	15	57	Juan Berenguer	12
12	Jim Palmer	21	35	Dan Spillner	15	58	Kirk McCaskill	12
13	Mike Moore	21	36	Dave Goltz	15	59	Mike Smithson	12
14	Bert Blyleven	20	37	Frank Viola	15	60	Neal Heaton	12
15	Dave Lemanczyk	19	38	Greg Harris	15	61	Steve Stone	12
16	Dave Stewart	19	39	Jose Guzman	15	62	Tom Candiotti	12
17	Dennis Eckersley	19	40	Mike Morgan	15	63	Vida Blue	12
18	Doc Medich	19	41	Roger Clemens	15	64	Bill Lee	11
19	Mike Boddicker	19	42	Gaylord Perry	14	65	Brad Havens	11
20	Storm Davis	19	43	Jim Bibby	14	66	Danny Darwin	11
21	Bret Saberhagen	18	44	Lamarr Hoyt	14	67	Dave Rozema	11
22	Dennis Martinez	18	45	Lary Sorensen	14	68	Dennis Leonard	11
23	Luis Tiant	18	46	Nolan Ryan	14	69	Jerry Garvin	11

Mike Flanagan
35 Hits

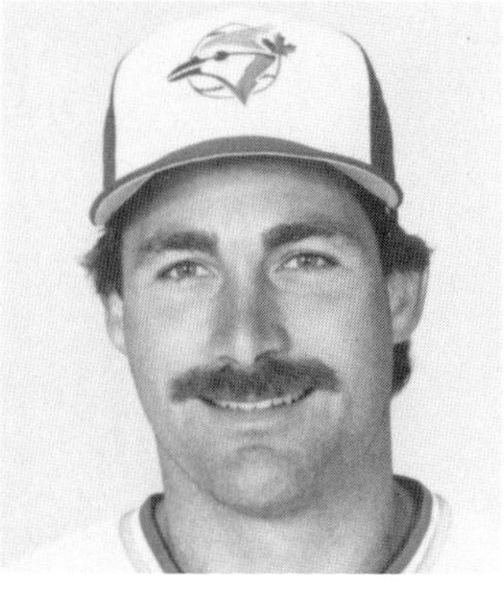

Dave Stieb
32 Hits

Jack Morris
31 Hits

Mike Torrez
25 Hits

	PITCHER	# OF HITS
70	Jerry Reuss	11
71	Luis Leal	11
72	Mark Eichhorn	11
73	Steve McCatty	11
74	Bill Swift	10
75	Doug Bird	10
76	John Cerutti	10
77	Mike Norris	10
78	Pat Dobson	10
79	Scott Bailes	10
80	Tom Underwood	10
81	Al Fitzmorris	9
82	Dan Quisenberry	9
83	Dave Righetti	9
84	Don Aase	9
85	Ed Figueroa	9
86	Jackie Brown	9
87	Len Barker	9
88	Mike Parrott	9
89	Nelson Briles	9
90	Reggie Cleveland	9
91	Rick Langford	9
92	Bill Long	8
93	Britt Burns	8
94	Charlie Leibrandt	8
95	Dennis Boyd	8
96	Dick Drago	8
97	Fritz Peterson	8
98	Geoff Zahn	8
99	Jeff Ballard	8
100	Jerry Koosman	8
101	Jesse Jefferson	8
102	Paul Hartzell	8
103	Phil Niekro	8
104	Rick Honeycutt	8
105	Shane Rawley	8
106	Steve Renko	8
107	Tim Stoddard	8
108	Vern Ruhle	8
109	Walt Terrell	8
110	Al Williams	7
111	Aurelio Lopez	7
112	Bart Johnson	7
113	Bill Gullickson	7
114	Bruce Hurst	7
115	Byron McLaughlin	7
116	Chuck Rainey	7
117	Dave Schmidt	7
118	Duane Ward	7
119	Gene Nelson	7
120	George Frazier	7
121	Jack McDowell	7
122	Jay Howell	7
123	Jeff Russell	7
124	Jeff Sellers	7
125	Jerry Reed	7
126	Jim Acker	7
127	John Farrell	7
128	Jon Matlack	7
129	Ken Holtzman	7
130	Mike Paxton	7
131	Ray Bare	7
132	Rich Gale	7
133	Rich Yett	7
134	Ron Romanick	7
135	Roy Smith	7
136	Steve Farr	7
137	Tom Murphy	7
138	Tom Seaver	7
139	Andy Hawkins	6
140	Ben McDonald	6
141	Bob Owchinko	6
142	Bryan Clark	6
143	Charles Hudson	6
144	Chris Codiroli	6
145	Chuck Finley	6
146	Curt Young	6
147	David Wells	6
148	Dick Bosman	6
149	Dick Tidrow	6
150	Don Kirkwood	6
151	Ed Vande Berg	6
152	Erik Hanson	6
153	Frank Wills	6
154	Greg Hibbard	6
155	Jerry Udjur	6
156	Jim Abbott	6
157	Jim Beattie	6
158	Jim Hughes	6
159	Joe Decker	6
160	Joel Davis	6
161	John Butcher	6
162	John Hiller	6
163	Ken Dixon	6
164	Kevin Brown	6
165	Lee Guetterman	6
166	Mark Williamson	6

Doyle Alexander
24 Hits

Larry Gura
24 Hits

Dan Petry
24 Hits

	PITCHER	# OF HITS
167	Marty Pattin	6
168	Matt Young	6
169	Mike Marshall	6
170	Ray Fontenot	6
171	Rich Gossage	6
172	Rick Sutcliffe	6
173	Scott Bankhead	6
174	Shawn Hillegas	6
175	Stan Bahnsen	6
176	Steve Busby	6
177	Steve Hargan	6
178	Tippy Martinez	6
179	Tom Burgmeier	6
180	Tom Henke	6
181	Wilbur Wood	6
182	Al Nipper	5
183	Bill Campbell	5
184	Bill Caudill	5
185	Bill Krueger	5
186	Danny Jackson	5
187	Dave Beard	5
188	Dave Roberts	5
189	Dennis Lamp	5
190	Dick Pole	5
191	Dock Ellis	5
192	Don Gordon	5
193	Don Sutton	5
194	Eric King	5
195	Gary Serum	5
196	Jeff Robinson	5
197	Jim Crawford	5
198	Joe Coleman	5
199	John Candelaria	5
200	Keith Atherton	5
201	Ken Schrom	5
202	Melido Perez	5
203	Mickey Lolich	5
204	Mike Brown	5
205	Mike Campbell	5
206	Mike Cuellar	5
207	Mike Henneman	5
208	Mike Jackson	5
209	Mike Mason	5
210	Mike Proly	5
211	Paul Gibson	5
212	Pete Filson	5
213	Pete Redfern	5
214	Ron Davis	5
215	Ross Grimsley	5
216	Sammy Stewart	5
217	Steve Ontiveros	5
218	Steve Trout	5
219	Tom Gordon	5
220	Allan Anderson	4
221	Bill Singer	4
222	Bob Ojeda	4
223	Bob Welch	4
224	Bobby Thigpen	4
225	Brian Holman	4
226	Charles Nagy	4
227	Charlie Lea	4
228	Chris Knapp	4
229	Dave Heaverlo	4
230	Dave Johnson	4
231	David Clyde	4
232	Dennis Rasmussen	4
233	Don Gullett	4
234	Don Schulze	4
235	Doug Corbett	4
236	Dyar Miller	4
237	Ed Farmer	4
238	Ed Hodge	4
239	Edwin Nunez	4
240	Francisco Barrios	4
241	Gerald Alexander	4

	PITCHER	# OF HITS
242	Greg Swindell	4
243	Jack Billingham	4
244	Jackson Todd	4
245	Jamie Easterly	4
246	Jim Kaat	4
247	Jim Slaton	4
248	Joe Johnson	4
249	Joe Slusarksi	4
250	John Leister	4
251	John Montague	4
252	Jose Bautista	4
253	Jose Nunez	4
254	Kenny Rogers	4
255	Luis Sanchez	4
256	Mark Fidrych	4
257	Mike Jeffcoat	4
258	Pat Underwood	4
259	Randy Johnson	4
260	Ray Burris	4
261	Rick Rhoden	4
262	Rick Waits	4
263	Rob Dressler	4
264	Rod Nichols	4
265	Roger Erickson	4
266	Rollie Fingers	4
267	Scott Aldred	4
268	Steve Comer	4
269	Steve Crawford	4
270	Tom House	4
271	Wade Taylor	4
272	Willie Fraser	4
273	Alan Mills	3
274	Bob Milacki	3
275	Bob Shirley	3
276	Bob Stoddard	3
277	Bob Tewksbury	3
278	Brad Arnsberg	3
279	Brian Allard	3
280	Cecilio Guante	3
281	Claude Osteen	3
282	Dale Mohorcic	3
283	Dan Schatzeder	3
284	Dave Fleming	3
285	Dave Hamilton	3
286	Dave LaRoche	3
287	Dave Tobik	3
288	Don Hood	3
289	Doug Bair	3
290	Ed Correa	3
291	Ed Halicki	3
292	Ed Whitson	3
293	Eddie Bane	3
294	Gene Garber	3
295	Greg Cadaret	3
296	Jack O'Connor	3
297	Jeff Musselman	3
298	Jeff Nelson	3
299	Jerry Don Gleaton	3
300	Jerry Johnson	3
301	Jim Barr	3
302	Jim Umbarger	3
303	Jim Willoughby	3
304	Jimmy Jones	3
305	Joe Grahe	3
306	Joe Niekro	3
307	Joey McLaughlin	3
308	John Denny	3
309	John Doherty	3
310	John Dopson	3
311	John Habyan	3
312	John Verhoeven	3
313	Jose DeLeon	3
314	Jose Rijo	3
315	Ken Brett	3
316	Ken Clay	3

Tommy John
23 Hits

Floyd Bannister
21 Hits

	PITCHER	# OF HITS
317	Les Straker	3
318	Mark Bomback	3
319	Mark Guthrie	3
320	Mark Leiter	3
321	Mel Stottlemyre	3
322	Mike Barlow	3
323	Mike Stanton	3
324	Neil Allen	3
325	Paul Mirabella	3
326	Paul Mitchell	3
327	Paul Reuschel	3
328	Pete Vukovich	3
329	Randy O'Neal	3
330	Rick Lysander	3
331	Roy Lee Jackson	3
332	Roy Thomas	3
333	Salome Barojas	3
334	Skip Lockwood	3
335	Steve Foucault	3
336	Steve Mingori	3
337	Steve Searcy	3
338	Tim Birtsas	3
339	Tim Conroy	3
340	Todd Burns	3
341	Todd Stottlemyre	3
342	Tom McCarthy	3
343	Wes Gardner	3
344	Adrian Devine	2
345	Alex Fernandez	2
346	Bill Mooneyham	2
347	Bill Scherrer	2

Pitching In!

	PITCHER	# OF HITS
348	Bill Wilkinson	2
349	Bob James	2
350	Bob Lacey	2
351	Bob Reynolds	2
352	Brian Fisher	2
353	Brian Holton	2
354	Bryan Harvey	2
355	Bud Anderson	2
356	Burt Hooton	2
357	Calvin Schiraldi	2
358	Cecil Upshaw	2
359	Dana Kiecker	2
360	Darrell Jackson	2
361	Dave Eiland	2
362	Dave Ford	2
363	Dave Frost	2
364	Dave Haas	2
365	Dave LaPoint	2
366	Dave Leiper	2
367	Dave McNally	2
368	Dave Rajsich	2
369	Dave Rucker	2
370	Dave Von Ohlen	2
371	Dennis Cook	2
372	Derek Botelho	2
373	Don Stanhouse	2
374	Doug Jones	2
375	Doug Linton	2
376	Drew Hall	2
377	Eric Bell	2
378	Eric Plunk	2
379	Eric Wilkins	2
380	Fernando Arroyo	2
381	Fred Holdsworth	2
382	Fred Martinez	2
383	Fred Toliver	2
384	Gary Ross	2
385	Greg Minton	2
386	Guy Hoffman	2
387	Jamie Moyer	2
388	Jeff Byrd	2
389	Jeff Little	2
390	Jeff Montgomery	2
391	Jeff Terpko	2
392	Jim Colburn	2
393	Jim Gott	2
394	Jim Kern	2
395	Jim Winn	2
396	Jim Wright	2
397	Joaquin Andujar	2
398	Joe Beckwith	2
399	John Barfield	2
400	John Curtis	2
401	John D'Acquisto	2
402	John Henry Johnson	2
403	John Pacella	2
404	Jose Mesa	2
405	Juan Agosto	2
406	Juan Eichelberger	2
407	Karl Best	2
408	Ken Forsch	2
409	Ken Kravec	2
410	Ken Patterson	2
411	Kevin Appier	2
412	Kevin Ritz	2
413	Kevin Tapani	2
414	Kip Young	2
415	Larry McCall	2
416	Len Whitehouse	2
417	Lerrin LaGrow	2
418	Luis Aponte	2
419	Luis Aquino	2
420	Mark Davis	2
421	Mark Portugal	2
422	Mark Thurmond	2
423	Mike Jones	2
424	Mike Schooler	2
425	Mike Willis	2
426	Moose Haas	2
427	Paul Kilgus	2
428	Paul Lindblad	2
429	Pete Broberg	2
430	Preston Hanna	2
431	Rich DeLucia	2
432	Rich Monteleone	2
433	Rick Aguilera	2
434	Rick Anderson	2
435	Ricky Steirer	2
436	Rob Murphy	2
437	Roger Moret	2
438	Ron Darling	2
439	Ross Baumgarten	2
440	Russ Swan	2
441	Scott Erickson	2
442	Scott Lewis	2
443	Scott Nielsen	2
444	Scott Scudder	2
445	Sergio Valdez	2
446	Skip Pitlock	2
447	Sparky Lyle	2
448	Stefan Wever	2
449	Steve Grilli	2
450	Steve Howe	2
451	Steve Olin	2
452	Ted Power	2
453	Terry Felton	2
454	Tim Leary	2
455	Tom Buskey	2
456	Tom Niedenfuer	2
457	Tom Walker	2
458	Tommy Moore	2
459	Willie Hernandez	2
460	Allan Ramirez	1
461	Allen Ripley	1
462	Andy McGaffigan	1
463	Balor Moore	1
464	Bill Castro	1
465	Bill Hands	1
466	Bill Laxton	1
467	Bill Stoneman	1
468	Bill Swaggerty	1
469	Bob MacDonald	1
470	Bob Veselic	1
471	Bob Wickman	1
472	Bruce Ellingsen	1
473	Bruce Kison	1
474	Bruce Robbins	1
475	Bruce Taylor	1
476	Calvin Jones	1
477	Carl Willis	1
478	Chuck Crim	1
479	Clay Carroll	1
480	Clay Parker	1
481	Craig Chamberlain	1
482	Craig McMurtry	1
483	Craig Mitchell	1
484	Curt Brown	1
485	Dale Murray	1
486	Dan Boitano	1
487	Darrell Akerfelds	1
488	Dave Geisel	1
489	Dave Gumpert	1
490	Dave Sells	1
491	Dave Wehrmeister	1
492	David Cone	1
493	David West	1
494	Denis Boucher	1
495	Dennis Kinney	1
496	DeWayne Buice	1
497	Dick Woodson	1
498	Dickie Noles	1
499	Diego Segui	1
500	Don Heinkel	1
501	Don Kainer	1
502	Don Robinson	1
503	Donn Pall	1
504	Dwayne Henry	1
505	Elias Sosa	1
506	Eric Raich	1
507	Ernesto Escarrega	1
508	Ernie Camacho	1
509	Fernando Valenzuela	1
510	Francisco Oliveros	1
511	Fred Howard	1
512	Gary Mielke	1
513	Gary Nolan	1
514	George Cappuzello	1
515	Gregg Olson	1
516	Howard Bailey	1
517	Jack Armstrong	1
518	Jack Kucek	1
519	Jack Lazorko	1
520	Jay Tibbs	1
521	Jeff Gray	1
522	Jeff Johnson	1
523	Jeff Kaiser	1
524	Jeff Parrett	1
525	Jeff Reardon	1
526	Jim Perry	1
527	Jim Ray	1
528	Jim Strickland	1
529	Joe Hesketh	1
530	Joe Hoerner	1
531	Joe Klink	1
532	Joe Skalski	1
533	John Mitchell	1
534	John Odom	1
535	John Tudor	1
536	Jose Roman	1
537	Juan Guzman	1
538	Keith Creel	1
539	Keith MacWhorter	1
540	Kevin Campbell	1
541	Kevin Hickey	1
542	Kevin Mmahat	1
543	Kevin Wickander	1
544	Kurt Knudsen	1
545	Lance McCullers	1
546	Larry Pashnick	1
547	Lee Smith	1
548	Les Lancaster	1
549	Lindy McDaniel	1
550	Luis DeLeon	1
551	Mark Clear	1
552	Mark Grant	1
553	Mark Huismann	1
554	Mark Lemongello	1
555	Mark Wiley	1
556	Matt Williams	1
557	Mauro Gozzo	1
558	Mike Armstrong	1
559	Mike Cook	1
560	Mike Fetters	1
561	Mike Gardiner	1
562	Mike Griffin	1
563	Mike Kinnunen	1
564	Mike LaCoss	1
565	Mike Loynd	1
566	Mike Rochford	1
567	Mike Trujillo	1
568	Mike Wallace	1
569	Mike Warren	1
570	Mitch Williams	1
571	Nate Snell	1
572	Odell Jones	1
573	Oswaldo Peraza	1
574	Paul Thormodsgard	1
575	Pete Harnisch	1
576	Pete Ladd	1
577	Phil Huffman	1
578	Randy Kramer	1
579	Randy McGilberry	1
580	Randy Scarbery	1
581	Rawly Eastwick	1
582	Ray Corbin	1
583	Renie Martin	1
584	Rich Hinton	1
585	Rich Thompson	1
586	Rich Wortham	1
587	Richard Barnes	1
588	Rick Jones	1
589	Rick Krueger	1
590	Rick Reed	1
591	Ron Reed	1
592	Roric Harrison	1
593	Rudy Seanez	1
594	Russ Springer	1
595	Rusty Meacham	1
596	Sammy Militello	1
597	Sandy Wihtol	1
598	Scott Chiamparino	1
599	Scott Kamieniecki	1
600	Scott Sanderson	1
601	Sid Monge	1
602	Stacy Jones	1
603	Stan Clarke	1
604	Stan Thomas	1
605	Steve Arlin	1
606	Steve Baker	1
607	Steve Barr	1
608	Steve Carlton	1
609	Steve Fireovid	1
610	Steve Luebber	1
611	Steve Rosenberg	1
612	Steve Shields	1
613	Steve Shifflett	1
614	Terry Forster	1
615	Terry Leach	1
616	Tim Drummond	1
617	Tim Lollar	1
618	Todd Frohwirth	1
619	Tom Bolton	1
620	Tom Griffin	1
621	Tom Makowski	1
622	Tony Arnold	1
623	Victor Cruz	1
624	Wayne Simpson	1
625	Willie Banks	1
626	Win Remmerswaal	1

Jim Clancy
21 Hits

Mike Moore
21 Hits

Jim Palmer
21 Hits

Bert Blyleven
20 Hits

Enjoy
Coca-Cola
CLASSIC
Trademarks ®
CATCH ONE AT THE GAME.
Can't Beat The Real Thing.
Official Soft Drink of Major League Baseball
©1992 The Coca-Cola Company. "Coca-Cola" and the
are registered trademarks of The Coca-Cola Company.

Robin
In Their

Compiled by

One year old Robin and pal "Apey."

MARION YOUNT, Robin's mother:

"To me he is like two Robins. There's the young man that goes on the ball field and then there is the son I've raised. Sometimes, it's hard to imagine them being the same person. With all that he has accomplished, it just doesn't seem real. I've always felt that as long as he is happy, I'm happy. I'm very proud of him, as I am of all my sons. They are all hard working, loving fathers and accomplished young men. What more can a mother want.

"Yet, what makes me the proudest of Robin is that he's still a nice person; with going into baseball at an early age and with all the things he has gone through during his career as a ball player, he is still nice little ole Robin.

"I know these accomplishments mean a lot to a lot of people. And I'm sure Robin understands them. But I know the most important thing to Robin is winning those ball games. God love him, he was a competitive little boy in Little League and I hope he never out grows it."

DICK RADENBAUGH, Umpired in the Sunrise Little League program and helped coach Robin as a youngster:

"There was something special about Robin Yount from the day he picked up a baseball glove. Even today, he sometimes leaves me spellbound. I visited with him during the off season and to me, he is still the same. All his success has not spoiled him. He treats me, my family and friends with all the kindness and respect one man can show."

PHIL YOUNT, Robin's father:

"Robin was competitive from the get-go. He always wanted to play with his brothers (Jim and Larry), who were much older than he was. They would invent games to play. They all would come up with some kind of game and Robin, well, he'd be right there. He'd get a big kick out of participating with them.

"By the time his brothers were playing little league, particularly Larry, Robin started out as a bat boy. Instead of picking up the bats, he'd be running around the bases and sliding into home plate. He was just copying the actions of the bigger boys. It was obvious to me that he would be interested in playing when he got a little older. When he got to be 8 or 9 years older, he was considered one of the better youngsters playing little league. He would either pitch or catch. They had a good program and were very successful.

"We knew once he got to high school that Robin had talent simply by the number of people that would come and watch him play. We weren't surprised that he was drafted to play professionally. His brother Larry was already playing (in the Houston Astros system), so, I guess, we were used to that. But we were surprised that he was called up to the big leagues when he was just 18 years old.

"We were there to support him in his first game on opening day (in 1974), but during that particular phase of growing up in the major leagues, it was all Robin. He showed me that he could handle the rough times, and there certainly were some for him in the beginning. I'll take some of the credit for instilling what he had in him. But, Robin took care of business himself.

"From day one, the message we tried to instill in all our boys was to give 100%. We told them to go at it hard. Do what the coaches tell you to do, without questioning. With Robin, because he was so competitive, winning was the most important factor of playing. That's probably why he always gave 100% effort.

"Robin has always put the team accomplishments ahead of his own. That is an honest feeling he has had since he first picked up a ball. He always was a team player.

"To me the fact that he has played successfully and has done a first class job is more important than all the measures used to determine the qualities of a player. To me, the fact that Robin has been able to go out there everyday and compete; earn the respect of the people he plays with and against; and earn the respect of those who come out to the ball parks across the country and watch him perform, are the most significant aspects of his accomplishments.

"Naturally, numbers come out of that success and longevity, but what makes me most proud of him is that he hasn't changed, regardless of all his accomplishments. Robin has done a first class job on the field and off. He has been able to do his job, stay quiet, come home and take care of his family. That's what I'm most proud of."

Yount Own Words

Mario Ziino

Robin's road to the big leagues began as a pitcher and catcher.

JIM YOUNT, Robin's oldest brother, a geologist:

"He was the most intense, competitive little kid I have ever seen. Nothing like his personality today. He hated to lose. I'm 10 years older than he is. But I can tell you that as the youngest of three brothers, Robin used to want to pal around with the older kids all the time. He always wanted to play with the big guys. He'd try to show you that he could play as well as the older kids. Maybe that is why he is so competitive.

"He has a great image and it's well deserved. He is a super person and a great family man. But I don't know how many people realize how much he competes within himself. He's constantly pushing himself to do better than he's done before. But he couldn't have had the success he has had if he didn't have that spark inside of him. I don't think I've known anyone quite like him. He is a driven person, yet, on the outside, he's very mild-mannered.

"The one thing about Robin, despite all the publicity, he'd sooner be low-key. That's why he loves playing in Milwaukee. He has told me that he couldn't imagine himself playing anywhere else. He can be himself and live a pretty normal life there.

"We all are very proud of him. But we've always been proud of him. He's worked hard at his profession and this accomplishment is a tribute to his ethics. Heck, it may even mean more to me than it does to him. But that's Robin. He's not orientated that way. He'd tell you that it's nice to reach 3,000 hits or be considered a MVP type-player or a Hall of Famer, but that's not why he played the game. He'd tell you he played to win games and reach the World Series."

LARRY YOUNT, Robin's brother and agent:

"I honestly believed that Robin was going to be a pitcher when he was in high school. He would visit me when I pitched in the Houston organization. At the time, I did not perceive him to be as good a shortstop as he turned out to be. I always thought he was going to be a pitcher. Obviously, I was wrong.

"The main thing that I've admired most about Robin is that very few people could start at 17 years old and basically wire themselves in monetarily and successfully in the major leagues; then later in their 30's have their heads on straight. He has had a remarkable ability to grow up in the major leagues and still treat others with respect. All of us can learn a lot from that.

"I know Robin has the ability as a professional athlete. But he also has the ability as a person. He's in a profession where quite a few things are handed to you. Things are done for you. He's been able to weed through all that. He never looks at things in the regard that it should be done for him. When something needs to be done, he does it himself.

"He is fortunate to have the physical talent better than most people and has the motivation to get things done. He works very hard and is very good at whatever he sets his mind to. He's lucky to have the ability and the stick-to-it type attitude to get the job done when most people would quit. Robin is everything I ever dreamed about. I feel privileged to be close to him."

CLEMENT COHEN, Robin Yount's coach in the Sunrise Little League program, Woodland Hills, California:

"I had Robbie for three years. He wasn't very big. But, I'll tell you he was an incredible youngster. Talent aside, Robin was a very special young man. He had a great attitude which I believe carried him on to his greatness.

"I remember that he was very unselfish. At nine, 10 and 11 years old, many youngsters are close in talent, but what set him apart was that as he got older he began to do things others couldn't. You know how kids that age have a tendency to wander, to not totally concentrate on drills and so forth, well, not Robbie. He would be leading the rest of the team in wind sprints. That's how he played. He played very hard. When he got on the field, it was all business. Get him off the field and he was a kid. He caught and pitched and played some at shortstop.

"I remember he was an all-star at age 11 and 12. As a 12 year old in 1968, he pitched in tournament games and we (the Yankees) came within an out of going to the Little League World Series at Williamsport, PA. During those years with Robbie, we were 55-2. That gives you an indication of the type of dedication he had. I tried to teach my kids to not be good losers, but good sports. Don't be happy you lost, but rather, congratulate the opposition for what they've done. Robbie was that way. A tough competitor, who hated to lose. But when he lost, he was a gentleman.

"Even to this day, his desire has not changed. He loves to play. He loves to win. He is a throw back to the old ball players. He'll go out and play hurt. He'll go out and play for his team. There are only a handful of players in the game today like that.

"And yet, among them, Robbie is very special. He doesn't look for the notoriety. He's very down-to-earth. Robbie is a very loyal guy. That is why he has had a good relationship with the Milwaukee Brewers and their fans. He has a special relationship with (Brewers President) Bud Selig, which is very unusual in today's game.

"I'm exceptionally proud of him as a human being. He is a very good person. Robbie used every aspect of the game to improve himself as a person. There are big leaguers who probably have more talent but less heart. Robbie has heart, talent and character. That is the great quality in him. That's part of his makeup and that's why he's a great ball player."

ROBIN YOUNT

A quarterback at age 9 in Pop Warner Football.

GORDON GOLDSBERRY, Baltimore Orioles, Special Assistant to the General Manager, former Brewers scout who signed Robin Yount in 1973:

"He was a plus-runner with a plus-arm. It turned out that he was a better hitter with more power than we anticipated. Each summer, when Robin's brother, Larry was away playing baseball (in the Houston Astros farm system), Robin would visit him for about a month. He was used to the routine, more so than 90% of the people who signed professional contracts, so he wasn't as scared or upset or nervous about playing at the minor league level than others had been. He was more advanced. I believe he spent one summer at Newark (Class A New York-Penn League) and because the Brewers lacked shortstops and because of his advancement, they (the Brewers) decided to let him play. He never gave up the job.

"He's a tremendous athlete. He's a scratch golfer, he races motorcycles and he's an intense competitor. He was so much more advanced - quiet, not boisterous - but a competitor. Everything he did was at 100%, which is not easy to do over a 162-game schedule. But he has always been in excellent shape. That's why he has lasted as long as he has.

"There is no question Robin will be in the Hall of Fame. He is one of the premier offensive shortstops to ever play this game. I hope they give him full credit for his shortstop abilities because that is what he should be known as."

RAY O'CONNOR, Robin Yount's baseball coach at Taft High School, Woodland Hills, California, who retired in 1991 following a 30-year career as a physical education teacher:

"My first impression of Robin, who was somewhat tall and lanky, was that he was very quick, but his skills were not refined. Consequently, as an 11th grader, he led the league in errors at shortstop, simply because he was so quick. He got to balls that he couldn't handle. I would laugh because no one else would be able to get to some balls that Robin did and it would cost him. Even through his first year of varsity baseball, I knew that this youngster had the tools. Robin was very dedicated to the game.

"He matured after that season. During that summer, he joined his brother, Larry, who was pitching in the Houston Astros farm system. Well, Larry was with Denver of the American Association and for about a month or so, Robin travelled with them. When he returned, he realized that he had the capabilities of performing like players at the Triple A level. I think, in his mind, he knew. There never was a doubt that he had the ability to play professionally, it was a matter of refining his skills.

"I tried to instill in Robin that the game was strictly a game of percentage. Everyday, after practice, I would stay out on the field with Robin and hit him ground balls. I'd tell him, 'Robin, I'm going to hit you 100 ground balls. If you make seven errors, then you're a .993 percentage fielder. So there is going to come a time in your life, you're going to make errors. You may even make three errors in a row. But you have to know in your own mind that you are a .993 fielder, so don't let it bother you. Nothing should bother you when you know you have the skills to play this game well.'

"I think it may have helped him a bit when he joined Milwaukee. I think he knew that they were going to hit balls to him, and yes, he would make some errors. He went in with that attitude. Robin had a tremendously strong arm, very quick wrists and was a heck of a competitor.

"His senior year, Robin was the Player of the Year in the Los Angeles area. I think he hit .478 and was definitely far-and-away the best player in Los Angeles. I remember there were as many scouts as fans at our ball games. And you know what, I don't think he was ever in awe of the fact that most of the scouts, scouts like Whitey Ford and Eddie Lopat, were there to see him play. At the time, I had a pitcher by the name of Bill Chamberlain, who was an all-city pitcher. When the scouts would talk to Robin, Robin would spend most of the time trying to convince these scouts to take a good look at Billy. That's the way he was.

"Robin, even at 18-years old, knew how to handle the media pressure. Robin was and is a very private person. He doesn't look for the notoriety. He's very humble. I remember the year he won the American League MVP award and he went home to visit his parents, the first thing he did was mow their lawn and take out their trash. He just likes to accomodate other people. He doesn't forget those that have helped him. I think he just doesn't feel that he is that important. He feels that he's just doing his job. Robin is thankful for his God given ability to play baseball.

"Granted, if Robin was playing in New York or Los Angeles, where there is more media attention, he would have gotten a lot of publicity because he is a super ball player. But he prefers Milwaukee above the rest. He's very loyal to the organization and that is why he has not gone the free-agent route.

"He told me many times, that he loves Milwaukee. He enjoys the organization, the fans and the lifestyle. So, you see, Robin is not a egotist. He's a good representative for the game. And, in my opinion, a Hall of Famer."

ROLAND LE BLANC, Milwaukee Brewers Special Assignments scout and former Brewers Scouting Supervisor, who signed Robin Yount in 1973:

"The main thing about Robin when I saw him back in high school was that he always went to the ball. He had a knack about being around the ball. He swung the bat well for a high school player. I remember he was also an above average runner.

"It's funny, I never really anticipate what a player will do once he reaches the big leagues. We scout so many youngsters and most don't get there. Heck, I never thought Robin would be a home run hitter and look what he did during his career. That's a credit to him. He built himself up. He was always a good worker. He certainly is a manager's ball-player. To come right out of high school and to do what he's done, it's quite an accomplishment. I've seen a lot of young talent over the years. I truly have not seen anyone like him since. He is special. He wanted to play. He wanted to be a big league player from the day he picked up a baseball mitt.

"Much of the credit of drafting Robin should go to Jim Baumer (the Brewers Director of Scouting at the time and later the club's General Manager). If I remember correctly, there was another youngster by the name of Richard Schubert, a pitcher, they were interested in. Jim made the right call on that, going after Robin.

"I remember the night before the draft, Jim and I talked about who we were going to draft. After our conversation, Jim made up his mind on Robin. It was the right choice, because this kid is going to the Hall of Fame when he's done playing."

YANKEE
YANKEE
YANKEE
YANKEE
YANKEE
YANKEE
YANKEE
YANKEE
YANKEE
YANKEE

Robin (far right, kneeling) with the Yankees of the Sunrise Little League.

It's What's Inside
That Counts.
© 1992 Miller Brewing Co., Milwaukee, WI
MILLER BREWING COMPANY
REMINDS YOU TO PLEASE:
THINK
WHEN YOU
DRINK
TM
Lite
Lite
Miller Lite. It's it and that's that.™

WILLIE MAYS, San Francisco Giants Instructor, Member of the 3,000 Hit Club and Baseball's Hall of Fame:

"Being in the National League, I really didn't get a chance to see Robin play very much. But what I do know about him is that he is a complete player. What made him one of the top players in the American League is his consistency. But durability is a key, too. He has played this game a long time and has been productive. That's what put him in a position to get 3,000 hits.

"He's not a pure hitter like a Rod Carew, who won a lot of batting titles, and he doesn't have the power like a Reggie Jackson and the speed like a Rickey Henderson, but he does have a little bit of everything. I know he drives in a lot of runs. That's important, too.

"In 22 years, I only won one batting title, but I was consistent. I hit over .300 with power and production.

"Being a centerfielder all my career, I can appreciate the fact that Robin went from shortstop to centerfield. I think that helped him a lot. You know, when you play shortstop, you're always in the game. Every play. But in the outfield, you can relax a little bit. That helps.

"I remember when Ernie Banks did that. He was a great shortstop for a long time with the (Chicago) Cubs. He moved to first base and became a great first baseman. That helped his career. But you know, natural athletes can do that.

"I know Robin won an MVP at shortstop then again, as a centerfielder. He's a natural. You see, that's what I mean about being consistent and durable.

"If I had a vote, yes, Robin Yount would go to the Hall of Fame when he's done playing. He's put up all the right numbers and getting 3,000 hits gets my vote."

A passion, Robin begins competitive motocross racing as a 13 year old.

REGGIE JACKSON, Oakland Athletics television analyst who was the California Angels rightfielder in the 1982 American League Championship Series against the Brewers and is a future Hall of Famer:

"I hope he plays until he is at least 40 years old. He has a good young body, a body he has always taken good care of. Players like Robin Yount are in that Hall of Fame mode. Can you imagine, of all the players that have played this game, more than 6,000 a year for over 100 years, only 160 or so are in the Hall of Fame. And here is a guy, Robin Yount, who exemplifies the qualifications and characteristics of a Hall of Fame player.

"On top of that, he is a wonderful person. I remember when he broke in as a wiry 18 year old shortstop who had great skills and potential. He really never embarrassed himself as a youngster. Even as he got older, seriously hurt his arm and moved to the outfield, he still played like an all-star and won an MVP award. He's a special player. The word superstar was first associated with Willie Mays because of the great player he was during his career. And now that Robin Yount has reached the 3,000 hit plateau, it's more or less, a stamp of approval of a player who fulfilled the criteria of a superstar."

HANK AARON, Atlanta Braves, Senior Vice President, former teammate of Robin Yount's, All-Time Home Run Champion, Member of the 3,000 Hit Club and Baseball's Hall of Fame:

"I've always liked him. I could see so many wonderful things happening to this young man. I always knew there was something special about Robin Yount as a baseball player. He has a special way of carrying himself. Somewhere in Robin Yount, I noticed a consistency that a lot of youngsters didn't have.

"He took his baseball very serious. I remember Robin wasn't flamboyant. He came to play. So I figured, if he stayed healthy, the success he has had would not be a surprise to me. Robin took it one day at a time, yet, I'm sure he now looks back and wonders where all the years have gone. I know, because I did. I'm sure Robin looks back, with pride, at his accomplishments. The memories will always be cherished.

"From day one, right through today, Robin gives the fans everything he's got. That's why he was in a position to get 3,000 hits. He's been able to hit and hit with some power. When you take into consideration that when he first came up he couldn't hit home runs and now, he's hit over 250 home runs in his career, that's pretty good. Now, he's one of only a handful of players to ever reach 3,000. Why, because he is a proud player. He has kept himself in excellent shape. And has worked hard. Let me tell you, when you work hard you can accomplish most anything you want. To me, Robin Yount is a blessing in disguise.

"I have often said, the greatest thing that ever happened to Milwaukee was that Robin Yount wanted to play his entire career with the Brewers. When I think of this franchise, I think of Robin Yount. That's the biggest tribute you can make to a player and to a club. It's something to be proud of. Robin is a product of this club. He came up through its farm system. He has blossomed into a great player, one of the greatest of his time. It's just a matter of time, before Robin Yount will be in the Hall of Fame."

Robin spent just 64 games at Newark in 1973 before joining the Brewers.

HARRY DALTON, Brewers Senior Vice President and former General Manager:

"He is a classic player in the sense that he has all the physical ability to play the game well. He has the ideal mental makeup. To me, Robin has always approached the game with the enthusiasm of a high school senior playing for the state championship. He comes to the ball park everyday and loves to put the uniform on. He loves to play the game. He has been a solid team player for as long as I've known him.

"For all the individual records, his effort has always been for the team to win. It puts him in a class with some of the great players I've had the pleasure of working with— Brooks Robinson, Frank Robinson and Nolan Ryan. Not only do these individuals have tremendous ability but also a tremendous desire for the team to win.

"Nothing about Robin's accomplishments amaze me. It's just a measure of how good he has been. Perhaps, he may not have won a batting title, but he has always been a consistent offensive force.

"He is an exceptional athlete which is a testimonial of his ability to move from shortstop to centerfield. He's a gifted athlete."

GEORGE BAMBERGER, Brewers manager from 1978-80; 1985-87:

"Let me tell you a story about Robin Yount. Back in 1989, a reporter from the (St. Petersburg) Times calls me and asks me to pick an all-star team. Well, the first person I think of is Robin Yount. Now this happened before the season even started. Robin goes on to earn the MVP award. At the end of the year, this reporter calls me back wondering how I knew Robin Yount would be such a great player. I told him, listen, I managed this man and he is the most perfect ballplayer a manager could manage. I know Robin Yount's ability. Heck, I wasn't just talking off the top of my head.

"It's true! Robin Yount is the finest player I ever had the privilege to manage. I'm talking about all the players I have come in contact with in all my 40-some years in the game. I can't say enough good things about Robin Yount, really. He was consistent. Listen, he was a great shortstop and outfielder. He's an excellent base runner. He has great baseball sense. He can hit and he can hit with power. There aren't too many guys in the game that can do all that.

"I've said this before, Robin Yount is my favorite player. Not only can he play but his desire and approach to the game is fantastic. He never complains. He's one man that if he hits the ball back to the pitcher will run hard to first base. He's not a loafer. You've got to like a guy like that.

"Without a doubt in my mind, Robin Yount is a Hall of Famer."

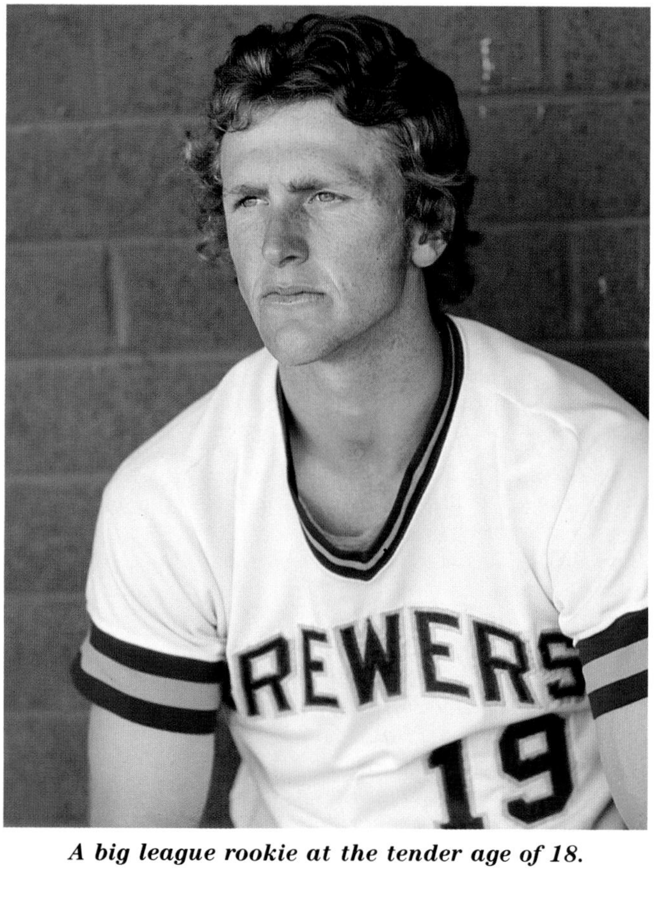
REWERS
19

A big league rookie at the tender age of 18.

BREWERS
19

Establishing himself as a major league shortstop.

TOM TREBELHORN, Brewers manager (1987-91):

"He has been a great timely ballplayer and has produced even through adversity. He has had shoulder surgery and back surgery and all the nagging injuries that can keep players out of the lineup or end their careers prematurely. Even through all that, he's ready to play every day. He's ready to play hard and give you everything he has. That symbolizes his career. His ability is easy to see, but the intangible factors, the will to play, the will to do well and the will to set an example of what a true major league player should be, that to me is Robin Yount.

"What I'll always remember and cherish about Robin Yount is that he wants to play and play well. He does not accept from himself or anyone else less than 100%. I'll remember him as the classic professional baseball player. He is a Hall of Famer with what he brings to the game - his attitude. He is the best player I've ever been around.

"There haven't been too many players who have been named the league's Most Valuable Player at two different positions and those others are in the Hall of Fame. How many other shortstops have done what he did? Those before him are in the Hall of Fame and those after will definitely go to Cooperstown. So, I don't doubt he'll someday be inducted.

"Robin Yount is a phenomenal example of American baseball. And, I think phenomenal examples of American baseball are in the Hall of Fame."

baseball

Fans favorite All-Star in 1983.

DEL CRANDALL, Brewers television announcer, who was Robin Yount's first manager in 1974:

"I remember he came down to spring training in 1974 with only 60 games of rookie ball under his belt. No one really anticipated that this young 18 year old would get a look. I was one of those people. But I remember standing behind the batting cage at Sun City one day watching him take some ground balls at shortstop. As I was watching him, I thought to myself that this kid had all the right moves. At that point, I picked up the fungo bat and began hitting him some ground balls. He showed a good arm and quickness.

"I went to Jim Wilson, who was our general manager at the time, and asked him if there was any reason why an 18 year old kid couldn't play shortstop for us? He couldn't think of a reason, so I played him.

"He handled the pressure well. He had his rough times like anyone else, but he hung in there. He showed no anger, no frustration. He looked like a young man meant to play the game. He had great makeup and great tools. He was a natural ball player. He didn't need any changing, just refinement. He had the confidence of a major leaguer without boasting about it. He was going to learn how to be an outstanding baseball player. To this day, he is no different than what he was years ago. He was destined to be a major league ball player. Not just a major league ball player, but a good one, who'll be a Hall of Famer when all this is done.

"Who could have ever projected that Robin Yount would get 3,000 hits, particularly back some 20 years ago. It's just like Henry Aaron. I played with Hank for a number of years in Milwaukee and I really never thought that this man would go on to break Babe Ruth's home run record. As time goes on, yes, you can see certain players begin to stand out.

"To me, Robin Yount is a Hall of Famer because of his contributions to the game. He has represented himself and the Milwaukee Brewers in the best way possible. Baseball and winning have been in the main thrust of his career, not individual statistics. Those things just come about because he has made the consistent contributions to this game. If players like Robin, who compile the records, don't end up in the Hall of Fame, something is wrong."

REWERS
19

Robin with his parents, Phil and Marion Yount.

PHIL GARNER, Brewers manager:

"When I saw him play 19 years ago, I remember saying to myself that there is something special about this kid's ability and determination. Today, he's the same. So many things are written and said about guys getting to the big leagues and changing. Their attitudes change. They get 'bigleagitis.' They rest on their laurels. The most refreshing thing about Robin is that from the first day I met him 19 years ago to today, he has not changed. He plays the game with the same intensity, the same determination and the same will to win as he did 19 years ago. In today's climate, it's a rarity. He is just one super player.

"Longevity and production over time are the two most important criteria to me to explain what a superstar should be. Robin has shown, time and time again, that he is one of the top, consistent producers in the game. You don't have to lead the league in hits to be considered among the greatest players. Success in this game is based on consistency. Any of us that have played it know how difficult it is to be consistent year-in-and-year-out. It's not difficult to have one good year and then three bad years, then one good year. The difficulty is maintaining a good level of play throughout your career. Robin has done it."

BOB (BUCK) RODGERS, California Angels manager and former Brewers skipper who led the club to its first post-season action in 1981:

"Robin Yount, is perhaps, one of the most disciplined players in the game today. Even after so many years in the league, he still works hard at perfecting his game. Robin Yount is a perfect example of a player going from one key position at shortstop to another key position in centerfield without a hitch. We take this for granted, but Robin Yount has always been able to do it all. He can run, he can hit, hit with power and play defense. This is what made him a great player."

STAN MUSIAL, St. Louis Cardinals Announcer, Member of the 3,000 Hit Club and Baseball's Hall of Fame:

"It's an achievement to be cherished forever. I'll never forget the day I got it and I'm sure Robin won't either. Robin Yount is a fine ball player, one I'm sure the people of Milwaukee are very proud of."

SAL BANDO, Brewers Senior Vice President-Baseball Operations, who played against Robin Yount in mid-70's and later with him when he closed out his career with Milwaukee:

"When I played against him, I noticed he had an untapped potential. I knew it would come out because of his attitude and his work ethic. I knew nothing would stop him from being the type of player he is.

"When I joined the Brewers that's when I really noticed how good he was. Each year, Robin got better and better. Robin reached his peak, as far as raw talent goes, in 1982 when he earned his first American League Most Valuable Player Award. After that, what I noticed more than anything else about him, was the fact that as he got older, he got smarter as a player. It wasn't strictly reflex or God given ability, it was a better understanding of how to get the most out of oneself when you may not be capable. By that I mean, Robin battled a serious shoulder injury that could have ended his career. But he learned to play with the injury. He learned to overcome the pain. He went from being an MVP shortstop to the outfield and had to learn a new position. He did, reaching another plateau in 1989 when he was named MVP, again.

"Here is a player, who had to make adjustments, and still performed up to his potential. You have to give him credit for doing that. Not too many players can do that. That is why I think Robin is as complete a player as I ever saw. He didn't win any batting titles. He didn't win any home run titles. He didn't win any RBI titles. But day-in-and-day-out he gave the effort. He was consistent. You ask any manager and he'll say, 'give me a player who goes out there everyday, produces everyday.' That's Robin Yount.

"Robin has had the ability to play, to stay fairly healthy and produce. That is what put him in a position to get 3,000 career hits. Consistency and longevity put Robin in that exclusive company."

WHITEY HERZOG, California Angels Senior Vice President, who managed the St. Louis Cardinals in the World Series against the Brewers in 1982:

"Robin Yount has always been a good ball player. He's been the kind of player, even when he came up as a shortstop and later with the tender shoulder, to be able to get a lot out of his ability. The true fact of a Robin Yount is not that he got 3,000 hits, but that he goes out there everyday and hustles. He does whatever it takes to win. He just plays the game of baseball the way it is supposed to be played."

BOB UECKER, Brewers Radio Announcer, who has broadcast Milwaukee baseball games over the last 22 years and has seen nearly every one of Robin Yount's hits:

"Robin is one of my dear friends. I've known him since his first day in a big league training camp. What has impressed me most about him is that from day one, this has been a game to him. Many of us who have played this game have at sometime felt it was a chore, a job. To Robin, it has always been a game.

"Awards and honors are secondary to Robin. What drives him is getting another opportunity to win a world championship. In 1982, guys like Robin and Paulie (Molitor) and Jimmy (Gantner) lost. They have been here all this time and would like one more shot at winning. That's what motivates Robin.

"Sure he has tried to downplay getting 3,000 hits. You know when you think about it, that's a big time career. I'm sure when it all sinks in, he'll be proud of his accomplishments, but he's a competitor and a competitor in this game strives for one thing, to be the best. And to be the best you want to be world champions.

"To me, Robin is in that category already. When I look at the company that he is in, guys like Joe DiMaggio, Stan Musial, Willie Mays, Henry Aaron - guys that I idolize - and some guys I never saw but know are the greatest the game has produced, I become awed by him. He is not an average player. He's a Hall of Fame player.

"His accomplishments will be looked at and measured by for generations to come. Baseball fans today are watching a Hall of Famer. They will remember a particular thing he did, a game they saw him play in.

"I admire him. He's a special player. A special human being."

The Yount Family: Robin and Michele with daughters, Melissa, Amy and Jenna, and son Dustin.

DAVE McNALLY, Baltimore Orioles pitcher who served up Robin Yount's first big league hit, on April 12, 1974:

"I remember it. I believe it was a ground ball up the middle. When was it? 1974? Wow! He was lanky back then and I knew he was brand new. He's been so great over the years. He can send me a thank you card (when he gets his 3,000th hit).

"It's so rare (to get 3,000 hits) for anyone. You don't think about how long this player or that player is going to last. At that age (back in 1974, when Robin was 18 years old), it was hard to fathom how long he would be in the majors. It's just fantastic what he's done.

"If it wasn't for me, Robin would have just 2,999 hits.

"Hall of Fame material? Absolutely!"

PAUL MOLITOR, Milwaukee Brewers teammate:

"At least not until lately has Robin received the national attention for being the type of player he has been for so long. Yet, the people in this organization, his teammates and those like Jimmy (Gantner) and myself, who played with him in the World Series, have appreciated Robin Yount for as long as he's been wearing the uniform. This recognition was long overdue. A lot of us realized a long time ago that Robin was going to be one of those select few to be in a position to reach that magical milestone. I remember that Robin was one of the youngest to reach 1,000, then 2,000, then 2,500 hits in a career. It came down to whether or not he would choose to continue playing. Fortunately, he did. So it was natural for him to be in a position to reach 3,000 hits.

"Notwithstanding, it still is amazing and exciting. Robin will down play it. That's Robin. But people, who know the game and the significance of his accomplishments will know what it means. I'm just proud to say that I've seen the majority of those hits and to have played with him. To have him for a teammate during my entire career in Milwaukee has definitely been a highlight. Just having the opportunity to watch him play, to learn from him by how he plays and approaches the game, has been a thrill. When you think of a perfect teammate, the characteristics of what he would have as far as the dedication to winning, the unselfishness, Robin Yount would be the person who meets those standards. I feel fortunate to have him as a teammate and friend for all my career.

"The Hall of Fame? There hasn't been a doubt in my mind for a long while. What he has meant to baseball and his accomplishments, whether it's the 3,000th hit, or his MVP's at two different positions, should be his ticket. Even by taking away all the statistical achievements, Robin has represented himself and the Milwaukee Brewers like a true Hall of Famer should."

PETE ROSE, Baseball's All-Time Hits Leader:

"Robin is a great hitter. He has a lot of talent and has been a very aggressive player. I know he has had fun playing this game. Coming up as a kid was a feather in his cap. He's been able to hang in there all these years. He's had his share of injuries, and yet, he has been able to continue with the consistency that it takes to get 3,000 hits.

"I remember getting my 3,000th hit and it's something I'll never forget. Unlike Robin, I won my share of batting titles and only missed 10 games during the decade of the 70's. But Robin is more of a run producer than I was. But reaching 3,000 hits is like a plateau-like 300 wins for a pitcher and 500 home runs for a slugger. Only super players can reach those plateaus. Robin and George Brett may be the last to reach this plateau for some time. First of all, a player has to have some luck from the stand point of playing in a lot of games. Most of the players that reached 3,000 hits have been aggressive players. Perhaps the most important criteria to reach 3,000 hits is consistency. A player in that position knows he's going to get the opportunity to get the hits, but he has to do it every year, not every other. Robin has been one of the more consistent hitters over the last two decades.

"There are a couple of others down the road that might have a crack at reaching 3,000 but everything has to work in their favor. It doesn't always happen. Guys today don't think of playing 18, 19 or 20 years anymore. They don't need to. Salaries have changed players and owners. I'm a firm believer that most of the longevity records-Cy Young's 511 victories, Nolan Ryan's strikeouts, my 4,256 hits and Henry Aaron's 755 homes-will not be threatened. Longevity, consistency and obviously, plenty of luck, make these records.

"In my opinion, any player who reaches these plateaus should be a Hall of Famer. Robin will make it on the first ballot. I know I'd vote for him. He deserves the Hall of Fame."

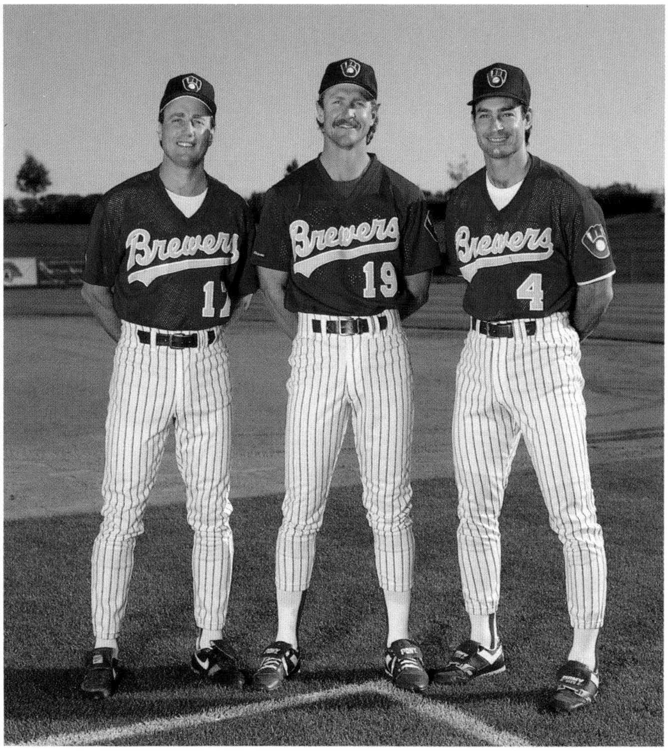
Brewers
17
Brewers
19
Brewers
4

Baseball's all-time hitting teammate-trio: Jim Gantner, Robin Yount and Paul Molitor.

JIM GANTNER, Milwaukee Brewers teammate:

"He's been consistent day-in-and-day-out. Never too high, never too low. He plays at one level whether things are going well or badly for him. He's very team oriented. I've known him for most of my playing career and he just wants to help his team win, help it get back to a World Series. Robin is a leader by how he approaches the game. I've seen him play hurt. But he's been a good example of a player who just loves to play this game. He's helped me during my career, too; I've learned from watching him play. We've had a great relationship over the years. I feel blessed to have played with and have known Robin and Paul (Molitor).

"As for Robin getting his 3,000th hit, I knew for a long time that he was going to get there. He's been playing a long time and hasn't missed too many games. If anyone in this game today was going to get 3,000 hits, it was going to be Robin. Robin is definitely a Hall of Fame player. He was a great shortstop, winning an MVP, then goes to the outfield and wins another MVP. And yet, for all the success he has had, Robin has no ego. He's down to earth. It's been my pleasure to know and play with Robin."

ROD CAREW, California Angels Batting Coach, Member of the 3,000 Hit Club and Baseball's Hall of Fame:

"I think from the time he came up, I noticed he knew how to play this game and play it well. The more you watched him, he just made things look easy. Even though he was young and taking his lumps early, he hung in there like a veteran. I don't think he'll realize the significance of attaining 3,000 hits for a while afterwards. It's just a great feeling that only a handful of us had the privilege of reaching. Yes, I am happy to welcome him into our group.

"Hitters like Robin, who show the longevity and consistency, that says something about the type of player he is. He is a great ballplayer who has adapted well. I'm happy for him because he is just a good person all around. I wish he would have gotten his hit against the Angels for a selfish reason. I personally would have liked to shake his hand to welcome him to the club."

AL KALINE, Detroit Tigers Announcer, Member of the 3,000 Hit Club and Baseball's Hall of Fame:

"A lot of players have the potential to reach 3,000 career hits, but to do so, you have to have everything going well for you. Robin was able to get to the big leagues at a young age. He became a regular quickly. He was a consistent hitter and lasted a long, long time. That's what has made Robin an outstanding player. Very few players have been able to go from one position to another and continue to excel. Robin has been an all-star shortstop and centerfielder. He's just an outstanding athlete.

"He looks very similar today as he did when he first broke in. He's in great shape, takes very good care of himself and he's been a natural player. Robin has been fortunate to stay away from the career ending injuries. He did have the shoulder problem that could have and would have ended most players careers, but again, Robin is an exceptional athlete, who wouldn't let it take his career away from him.

"Robin is a lot like me. He has been happy here (in Milwaukee) as I was in Detroit. People always told me that if I had played in New York, I'd be a better known player. They say the same about Robin. If he had played in a major market, they'd name candy bars after him, too.

"There is no question in my mind that Robin will go (to the Hall of Fame) on the first ballot. He'll be there with or without reaching 3,000 hits. You are talking about a player who was a great shortstop - one who was named the league's Most Valuable Player - then went to the outfield and became a great centerfielder - again, being named MVP. Getting 3,000 hits, however, will lock it up for him."

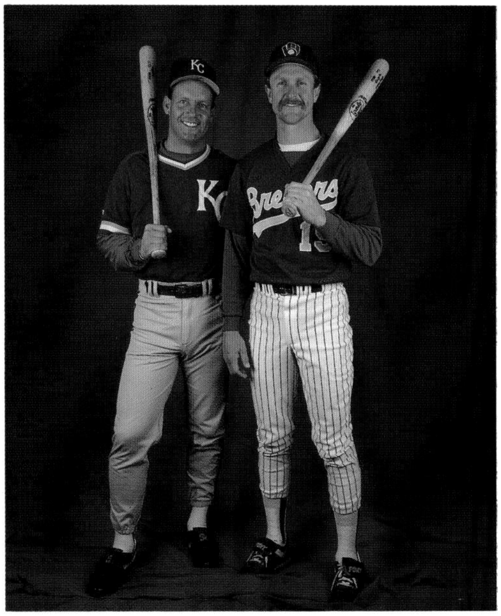

George Brett and Robin Yount.

Winston
ROBIN YOUNT DAY
BREWERS
19

An appreciative Robin acknowledges Brewers fans at County Stadium on Robin Yount Day.

GEORGE BRETT, Kansas City Royals, the next player to collect 3,000 career hits:

"I've always admired Robin. I don't really look at him as a player, but more as a friend. Obviously, he has been a tremendous player over the years to amass the statistics that he has and to stay with the Brewers for as long as he has. When someone asks me about Robin, the first thing I say is that he is a friend of mine.

"I remember having a conversation with Robin the year he was eligible to become a free agent and we talked about it. I can tell you one reason why he stayed in Milwaukee - the Brewers have been very good to him. The reason I've stayed in the Royals organization for 21 years is that they've been good to me. You know, you might not see it very much anymore because of free agency, but the Royals and Brewers have shown loyalty to us and likewise, we to the team. We both grew up in Southern California. I dreamt of playing someday with the Los Angeles Dodgers or California Angels, just to be closer to family. I'm sure Robin has felt the same way. But when push came to shove, the loyalty factor came into play, for both of us.

"Another advantage we've had was playing in a smaller market. We don't have to put up with all the hype. We don't have to deal with all the outside attention. We can just play baseball. It makes it all a lot easier for us. I can't imagine playing in New York or Los Angeles or Chicago. It would be too distracting for me and I don't think I would have had the type of seasons I've had if I was in those big markets.

"Obviously, getting 3,000 hits would be the icing on the cake as far as the Hall of Fame is concerned. It's definitely a feather in your cap. We know that only 16 players have reached 3,000 hits. But, Robin has accomplished a few things that fewer have accomplished - winning the MVP at two positions. Likewise, I've done a few things that most others haven't.

"I'll be honest with you, I'm not playing this game aiming for the Hall of Fame. I'm sure Robin feels the same way. Don't get me wrong, it would be nice to make it. We are no different than anyone else. But we don't go out and try to make it. We play for the love of this game. We play to help our teams win. We play because we enjoy it. If your teams wins, you have fun and you have a good enough career, then you'll be invited into the Hall of Fame."

KENESAW MOUNTAIN LANDIS
MEMORIAL BASEBALL AWARD
MOST
VALUABLE PLAYER
AMERICAN LEAGUE
ROBIN YOUNT

A proud moment came in 1989 when Robin accepted his second MVP award from Brewers President Allan H. (Bud) Selig.

ALLAN H. (BUD) SELIG, Brewers President:

"He has meant a great deal to this organization. He epitomizes, this city and franchise. He has conducted himself with dignity and class. He is everything you would want, not only as an athlete, but as a person. Far more importantly, the thing that stuck with me, from the very first day I met him, is what a wonderful young man he is. And he has never changed.

"He is a focused athlete, who comes to play, plays hard every day and represents his city and team magnificently. There is no question in my mind that when he goes to the Hall of Fame, he'll go as Yount of the Brewers and I will be prouder of him as a human being than clearly his baseball exploits which are impeccable.

"I knew he was someone special. You could see that, you could sense that as the years went by. But this summer was remarkable. Day after day he passed players that are a paragon of this sport. He passed players such as Lou Gehrig, Joe DiMaggio, Ted Williams, it's a great story. This is something many of us may never see again.

"In an age, in an era where there is so much cynicism relative to a professional athlete, a Robin Yount is refreshing. He plays the game the way it was played 20, 30 and 40 years ago. I don't mean to sound like an old-timer, but that is a great compliment.

"When you think he has been here (in Milwaukee) for all these years, his entire career and never caused this organization a bit of a problem, he is a credit to his profession. I feel about him and his family as I do about my own family. It has been a wonderful relationship. It has been the type of relationship you would wish there was more of, not only in sports, but in the entire world.

"You can ask hundreds of players, not only those that have played with him, but those that played against him, and they would tell you how much they respect him. I guess, I have to say, how can you not respect him?"

JOSE MESA, Cleveland Indians Pitcher who served up Robin Yount's 3,000th career hit:

"When you have a player like that who can get 3,000 hits in his major league career all I can say is he is one of the greatest. I wasn't looking to give up the 3,000th hit ball but there's nothing I could do about it. I threw him two fastballs in a row and he hit them good. I'm happy for him. He's one of the greatest to play this game. You have to give him credit."

The Legend Lives On

CREDITS

MARIO J. ZIINO, Editor
JON GREENBERG, Assistant Editor
TOM SKIBOSH, Assistant Editor
LAUREL PRIEB, Associate Editor
SCOTT SHEFF, Media Relations Intern
ANDY BAGGOT, Wisconsin State Journal
KANDY STAMBORSKI, Artist
DIANA CRAMER, Cover Design
LARRY STOUDT, Photography
VAL MEYER, Photography
RON MODRA, Photography
DAN JOHNSON, Photography
PAUL ROBERTS, Photography

SPECIAL THANKS

PHIL & MARION YOUNT
LARRY YOUNT
PAUL BANIEL
CLEMENT COHEN
JIM KAAT
JOE KENNEDY
DENNIS SELL
BILL HAYES
JERRY GROSS

ACKNOWLEDGEMENTS

BOB MILLER, Balitmore Orioles
TIM MEAD, California Angels
MATT FISCHER, San Francisco Giants
BRIAN BARTOW, St. Louis Cardinals

COVER DESIGN

RISSER COLOR SERVICES, INC., Milwaukee

PRINTER

DELZER LITHOGRAPH CO., Waukesha, WI

SOURCES

The Baseball Encyclopedia (Seventh Edition), edited by Joseph L. Reichler

The Baseball Chronology edited by James Charlton

The Baseball Hall of Fame

The Ballplayers (First Edition) edited by Mike Shatzkin

ISBN 0-9634967-0-0

"I'm not very good at making speeches, but I sure can ride a motorcycle."

—Robin Yount

Bre